Collector's Encyclopedia of
NIPPON
PORCELAIN

Identification & Values

Sixth Series

Joan F. Van Patten

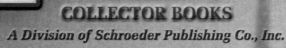

COLLECTOR BOOKS
A Division of Schroeder Publishing Co., Inc.

The current values in this book should be used only as a guide. They are not intended to set prices, which vary from one section of the country to another. Auction prices as well as dealer prices vary greatly and are affected by condition as well as demand. Neither the author nor the publisher assumes responsibility for any losses that might be incurred as a result of consulting this guide.

On the cover:

Front cover, lower left: Molded in relief vase, 8¾" tall, blue mark #47, $1,000.00 – 1,200.00.
Upper right: Wine jug, 11" tall, blue mark #47, $1,300.00 – 1,450.00.
Back cover, upper photo: Floral vase, 10" tall, green mark #52, $1,600.00 – 1,900.00.
Lower photo: Humidor, 7½" tall, blue mark #52, $700.00 – 825.00.

Cover Design: Terri Hunter
Book Design: Karen Geary

Searching for a Publisher?

We are always looking for knowledgeable people considered to be experts within their fields. If you feel that there is a real need for a book on your collectible subject and have a large comprehensive collection, contact Collector Books.

COLLECTOR BOOKS
P.O. Box 3009
Paducah, Kentucky 42002-3009
www.collectorbooks.com

Copyright © 2001 by Joan Van Patten

Contents

About the Author

⌣·━━━━━━━━━━━━━━━━━━━━·⌣

Joan Van Patten is the author of *Collector's Encyclopedia of Nippon Porcelain, First* through *Fifth Series, Nippon Price Guide, The Collector's Encyclopedia of Noritake, First*

and *Second Series, Celluloid Treasures of the Victorian Era* and *Nippon Dolls and Playthings*, all published by Collector Books. She is presently working on *Collector's Encyclopedia of Nippon Porcelain, Seventh Series.*

She has written hundreds of trade paper and magazine articles and is a contributor to *Schroeder's Antiques Price Guide.*

Joan has been on the board of the INCC (International Nippon Collector's Club) since its inception. She served as its first president and was also the co-founder. She has served as a director of the club for many years. Joan edited and published the *Nippon Notebook* and the *INCC Newsletter* for five years. She has lectured on the subjects of Nippon, Noritake, and celluloid throughout the United States.

The research of antiques and collectibles, travel, and volunteer work are other major interests of the author.

Acknowledgments

The first people I want to thank are Billy Schroeder and the great staff he has working at Collector Books. Billy has again approved another book in this series and I am extremely grateful to both him and his father, Bill, who published my first books. Lisa Stroup, my editor, and Amy Hopper, her assistant, are wonderful to work with and I am always so pleased at how they get these books to turn out so beautifully. My sincere thanks go to Billy and everyone on the staff at Collector Books for all their help.

I have received an abundance of photos and information from collectors and researchers all over the United States and even Japan. In fact, so much information has been obtained that the Seventh Series will soon follow this book. It's difficult to believe that so many new and wonderful items keep appearing on the Nippon market!

Mark Griffin and Earl Smith provided many wonderful photos for both the Fourth and Fifth Series, and when I asked them for photographs this time, I thought that they surely couldn't have many more new items to share, but was I wrong! They sent me hundreds of photos of fantastic items and Mark even volunteered to write the chapter on Nippon patterns, designs, decors, and scenes as well. Clement Photographic Services, Inc. in Fort Myers, Florida, took all their wonderful photos, and I am extremely grateful for the wonderful job they did. Many of Mark's and Earl's photos are featured in this book, and the remainder will be shown in the next. Earl and Mark have the most wonderful collection of Nippon porcelain that I have ever seen and are always willing to help in any way. They are the two most "dedicated" collectors I have ever encountered. They not only enjoy the "hunt" for items but are extremely knowledgeable in the Nippon field as well. Thanks go to both of you for all the work you did and for your help with pricing which is an almost impossible task.

My friend Keishi Suzuki of the Noritake Co. is always there to fulfill most any request I have. In this book I was able to include photos of many beautiful old artist renderings that are stored in the Noritake Co. archives in Nagoya. Keishi not only sent me these wonderful photos but also many photos of the exterior and interior of the Noritake Co.

factory and museum. Thank you, Keishi, not only for this information but also for being such a gracious host when I visited Japan.

Tony Kawamura, also from the Noritake Co., sent me the historical information you will find in the Noritake Co. chapter. The Noritake Co. and their employees have been so helpful with information, and I want to take this opportunity to thank them. Nippon is my favorite "stuff" and this is the company that produced most of it.

Keishi also arranged for permission to have the information on the Japanese kimono dresses to be printed in this book. The Nijoh Murachachi Co., Limited is now designing gorgeous kimonos using the old Noritake designs. Each is breathtakingly beautiful, and it's very exciting to see these old designs being used on the new kimonos. Wouldn't one of these kimonos look great placed next to the original item?

Ikuo Fukunaga (from Morimura Bros.) allowed me to print some of the historical information he gathered and presented at an INCC (International Nippon Collectors Club) convention. The Morimura Brothers Company played a big part in not only the early manufacture of these items but also their distribution in the United States. Thank you, Mr. Fukunaga.

Deborah Egan of the S&H Company provided me with much of the information I gathered on that company. She was very generous when I visited her at the New York City office and allowed me to view and photograph the old Rolodex, which held cards featuring the Nippon premiums given by the company years ago.

Frieda Van Winkle is a portrait specialist and was kind enough to view many photos of ladies featured on Nippon wares that I mailed to her. She confirmed my identification of these women and also provided some interesting information on a few. Thank you, Frieda.

Viola and Peter Zwern sent me the old newspaper article on Sophie Potozki. Is she or isn't she Anna Potocka? That's the question. Thanks to both of you for sharing this information with readers of this book and adding a little mystery to the lady.

Don Wright researched the information found on the Northwestern Indian pieces. His bizarre item was the first that I had ever seen although several more have popped up on the market since then. They are so unusual, and I wish to thank Don for bringing them to my attention and allowing them to appear in this book.

My good friend, Linda Lau, supplied several photos plus many of the revised and new back-stamps found on dolls in this series. Linda and I worked long and hard gathering information and photos for our book, *Nippon Dolls and Playthings*, and it's our hope that readers will purchase a copy and also discover the "small" world of Nippon. More than 600 different Nippon dolls, feeding dishes, children's tea sets, and toys are featured, and it is the definitive book on this subject.

Lewis and BJ Longest again took many photos of not only their own collection but those of several other collections. Lewis is a professional photographer, and both he and BJ have always been so helpful whenever I have asked a favor of them. They sent me wonderful photos! Some will appear in this book, and some will appear in the next. Thanks so much for all your help but most of all for just being so very nice.

Dawn Fisher opened up her home and allowed Linda Lau and me to photograph anything and everything in her collection of dolls for our *Nippon Dolls and Playthings* book. While I was there I also spotted her rooms of Nippon porcelain and was allowed to photograph many of these items as well. Dawn is a gracious hostess and a dedicated collector. My own Nippon collecting has enabled me to meet so many wonderful people and Dawn certainly falls into that category.

Ken Schirm sent me a large package of photos again this time, and readers will get to enjoy some of his treasures. I counted on him for photos in the last two books and now he's helped with both this book and the next. Ken's specialty is collecting wall plaques, but he also purchases other quality items as well. Thank you, Ken.

Lewis and BJ Longest took Bob and Maggie Schoenherr's photos, and I was delighted to see what new items they had found since the Fifth Series had been published. They didn't disappoint me and many of their items are featured in the following pages. Maggie and Bob are very involved in the field of Nippon collecting and can always be counted on when you need help with a book. Thank you so much for all your work and photos.

My good friends, Jess Berry and Gary Graves, send me photos of each new find, and I get to share in their delight soon after they make a purchase. Our friendship goes back a long way, and they are two people I consider to be very, very special. They have helped me with more projects than I can even remember, and I consider myself lucky to be their friend. Thanks again to both of you.

Janet and Bob Bing-You didn't want any special thanks in this book, but I do want to let them know how much I appreciate the many photos and descriptions they sent. More of their photos will be shown in the Seventh Series.

Frank and Ruth Reid are such a charming couple, and when asked to submit photos, they did so promptly. I really enjoy being in their company and want to say thank you so much for helping with this book.

Jack and Lisa Landrum also sent wonderful photos. Once you meet Jack and Lisa, you never forget them. They're both outgoing, a lot of fun, and so willing to help out with whatever you ask them to do. They not only love Nippon, but anyone who crosses their path! Thank you both.

David Bausch's specialty is collecting items featuring old automobiles and airplanes. David helped with information and photos in a previous book, and in this series I have featured some of the wonderful items he has found which feature old automobiles portrayed on Nippon. These are extremely difficult to find, and I want to thank David for his contribution.

Joe and Cheryl Meese also answered the call for photos, and a few of their items are included in this book. Thank you both.

I'd also like to thank the following people who supplied photos for the Sixth Series: Kathy and David McElrea, Jean Roberts, Jean and Craig Cole, Judy Boyd, Chuck Dillon, Nat Goldstein, Erik and Elaine Lunde, Polly Frye, Doris and George Myers, Lee Smith, Todd and Karen Lawrence, Gloria Addison, Brian and Yvonne Hurst, Terri Kempe, Deborah Ridden, and Gary Harkness. Because of the contributions of these people this book has become a reality and hopefully will give other collectors many hours of enjoyment. Thanks to all of you.

Introduction

"Wonder is the beginning of wisdom"
Chinese Proverb

A true collector wants to know the what, when, why, and where of the things he or she collects and as a result is also collecting history. The *Collector's Encyclopedia of Nippon Porcelain, First* through *Sixth Series* is an attempt to not only cover the history of Nippon items but also to help collectors refine their collecting skills so that fewer mistakes are made.

Thousands of wonderful items have been featured from lowly sugar bowls to palace urns. Some have had unusual uses and these too have been described. Old catalog ads have been included as well. It's been said that the only thing more expensive than education is ignorance, and it's the hope of this author that readers of these books will not just look at the beautiful pieces that are featured but will spend the time to really *read* the books.

Many people have contributed not only their photos but also their expertise and knowledge. It's unbelievable just how much new information has been discovered since the first book was published in 1979. Each time I start a new book I always wonder if there really are any more new and great items to be photographed, and every time collectors send me photos of more fantastic pieces.

Something readers need to keep in mind when viewing the photos is the description of the item(s). How tall or wide is the piece? The majority of items are shown individually in the photos so that readers can get a good close-up of the piece. Many times a couple of inches in height will be the only difference, and this does not seem like much of a difference when one reads the description. However, when placed next to each other, a 10¼" vase may seem very small next to a 24" one. In Photo 1, the vase looks normal in size but appears tiny sitting next to one two feet in height, see Photo 2.

Photo 1

Photo 2

The plates in Photo 3 are decorated with the same pattern but are found in different sizes. Naturally the larger one will be more expensive than the smaller one and collectors must keep this in mind when purchasing items. Although the item may appear to be very big in size in one of these books, it may really be very small when viewed in person.

Photo 3

Photo 4

Workmanship is also very important. Perhaps that statement should be clarified — good workmanship is always one of the first things to look for in an item. Also, ideally the items should be free of cracks, chips, hairlines, worn gold, etc. Because it is not always possible to find perfect or near perfect pieces, the price should at least reflect this when imperfections are found on the items.

My advice is to always buy the best quality possible. There will always be mediocre items in our midst but the truly wonderful collections consist of fine quality items.

Hand-painted work is preferable to decals except in the case of the portrait pieces. How can you tell if an item is hand painted or a decal? Decals are made up of tiny dots and can be viewed with the aid of a small magnifying glass. Hand-painted pieces will show brush strokes and truly are works of art, see close-ups of hand-painted work in Photos 4–8.

Moriage decorated wares are very desirable. The close-up Photo 9 of a moriage piece shows just how much thicker the clay slip has been applied as compared to the Wedgwood imitation shown in Photo 10.

Different types of material were used on tapestry items, and in Photo 11 you can see that a coarser material was placed on the piece. Photo 12 shows where a finer texture was used and so does 13, which also has a moriage owl that was applied on top of the tapestry medallion.

Photo 14 is a close-up of coralene decoration. Colorless glass beads were placed over the painted decoration and gave a plushy luminescence look to the item.

Photo 5

Photo 6

Photo 7

Photo 8

Photo 9

Photo 10

Photo 11

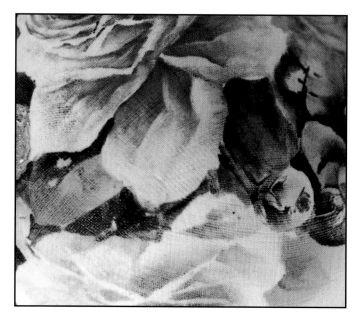

Photo 12

Photo 13

Photo 14

Photo 15

Gold overlay is featured in Photo 15 and appears to be quite thick. Actually the piece is decorated with heavy clay slip and then painted gold to give the appearance of a thickness of gold.

In Photo 16, we also see heavy gold decoration and beading. Photos 17 – 19 show aqua beading on a gold background, gold beading on a gold background, and gold beading on a brown background.

Relief molded or blown-outs (as they are commonly called) have a three-dimensional look. The pattern is raised up from the background. This is all accomplished in the mold and is not applied work, see Photos 20 and 21.

Collectors will sometimes find that some designs or pictures are in what we call mirror image (facing each other) that is true of the Christmas deer (elk) shown in Photo 22. Some urns and vases are also found in mirror image, but the majority of these have a United Kingdom backstamp on them.

Without proper information, mistakes can be made. One new collector told of the time when she threw out the ugly metal insert she found with a ferner, see Photo 23. She didn't know that the insert made the item more valuable. It's too bad she didn't at least store the insert as it does increase the price. Most collectors are delighted to find a complete item. Another collector thought he had a damaged

vase when he saw that it had been bolted together and was offering to sell it at a discounted price due to this "flaw." He didn't know that it was a bolted two-piece urn (Photo 24) and not damaged at all!

Old, original boxes are wonderful to find and definitely add to the price. The child's set shown in Photos 25 and 26 is marked Nippon and the box says Made in Japan. This is a truly an unusual find since it was once intended for child's play.

Collectors need to lift up the covers on items to see if there is damage as well as to see if a piece might have held a sponge long ago as shown in Photo 27. Although the article in Photo 28 looks like a tall cracker jar, it is in actuality a humidor. Knowing this gives the collector an edge, as the price will almost always be higher for a humidor than for a cracker jar.

Odd pieces pop up all the time, and the vase in Photo 29 looks as though two different pieces have been glued together. The design on top does not go with that on the bottom, and you have to wonder why it was decorated in this manner. It goes to show there's something for everyone.

Some collectors just do not have the space for large collectibles, and for those with limited resources or space, a suggestion might be to collect small vases, toothpick holders, hatpin holders, or even

Photo 16

Photo 17

Photo 19

Photo 18

Photo 20

Photo 21

Photo 22

Photo 23

Photo 24

Photo 25

Photo 26

Photo 27

Photo 28

open salts. One collector has managed to find a variety of small open salt dishes and part of her collection is shown in Photo 30.

This Sixth Series is filled with wonderful photos and new information. All types of items and decoration have been included. There's an old Chinese proverb that says "every book must be chewed to get out its juice," and it's my hope that collectors will find this book to be a feast!

Photo 29

Photo 30

History of Noritake Company, Ltd.
(Provided by the Noritake Company, Ltd.)

The founder of Noritake was Baron Ichizaemon Morimura who was born in 1839 to a family of merchants who acted as purveyors to feudal lords. In 1860, when he was twenty years old, the shogunate decided that a delegation needed to be sent to the United States to return the courtesy visit of Commodore Perry. Baron Morimura was ordered to change Japanese money into American coin in the Yokohama foreign concession for the delegation to carry to the United States.

The Japanese money to be exchanged was gold coin of high purity, while the currency to be received was coin of very low quality called Mexican silver.

Baron Morimura felt that it was a great loss to the country to allow gold of such high purity to flow out of Japan and spoke about the matter to Yukichi Fukuzawa, one of the great leaders in the modernization of new Japan from the feudal shogunate governing era. Fukuzawa told Morimura that it was necessary to promote export trade so that the gold that went out of Japan would flow back into the country.

Ichizaemon Morimura and his young brother, "Toyo" founded Morimura Kumi (Morimura Co.) at Ginza in Tokyo in 1876, and in the same year, Toyo formed a Japanese retail shop "Hinode" (later this became Morimura Bros. Inc.) at 6th Avenue, New York City. Then the two brothers started a trade business between Tokyo and New York and exported traditional Japanese style pottery, bamboo works, and other Japanese gift items and so-called Japanese sundry goods to the United States. This business transaction was the first trade between Japan and the United States after Japan opened its door with the Western countries.

During expansion of its export business, Morimura Bros. decided to change from a retail to a wholesale business and to concentrate on ceramics. Thus Nippon Toki Kaisha (later this became the Noritake Co., Limited) was founded on January 1, 1904, at Noritake village which is the present site of the main factory. This factory's primary purpose was manufacturing and exporting high quality china mainly to the United States. Since then, the United States has been the greatest supporter and biggest customer for Noritake.

The founders were Ichizaemon Morimura, Mogobei Okkura, Saneyoshi Hirose, Yasukata Murai, Kazuchika Okura, and Kotaro Asukai. The technique to manufacture high quality dinnerware was mastered in the 1910s, and Noritake adopted a streamlined mass-production system in the twenties and thirties and enjoyed the high reputation of Noritake china all over the world.

In the course of growth during the early period, Noritake started to research the construction of the sanitary ware and insulator divisions within the company. Later, the sanitary division became independent from Noritake in 1917. It was named Toyo Toki Kaisha Ltd. (presently Toto Limited) and is known as the biggest sanitary ware and related metal fitting manufacturer in Japan. The insulator division of Noritake also became independent from Noritake in 1919, later splitting into two companies in 1936. One is known as NGK Insulator Co., Ltd., the world's largest insulator manufacturer; the other is NGK Spark Plug Co., Ltd., which is one of the top manufacturers of spark plugs in the world.

In 1939, Noritake, which had been doing extensive research on abrasive grinding wheels, decided to mass produce bonded abrasive products. The company utilized its longtime experience with its knowledge of ceramics in making this decision.

During World War II, the Noritake factory produced abrasive grinding wheels for heavy industries instead of chinaware. Although Noritake's old main office building was burned in World War II, the factory buildings suffered almost no damage. Therefore, Noritake could start the production of chinaware sooner than other factories. However, the quality of china was not up to pre-war standards because of the lack of high technology and lack of superior materials and the equipment shortages at that time. In order to maintain the reputation of Noritake China, which meant quality products, the trademark "Rose China" was adopted temporarily before a satisfactory level of quality was restored. In 1948, the trademark "Noritake" was employed again.

In November 1947, Noritake Co., Inc. of the United States was incorporated in New York City, starting a chinaware wholesale business with major department stores and specialty stores. During the course of resumption of foreign trade with the United States and other countries in and after 1948, Noritake expanded itself extensively to become the largest chinaware manufacturer in the world. The new Miyoshi dinnerware plant was completed in 1965 in the eastern end of Nagoya. Noritake also improved its porcelain formula and a new production technique for fine china, bone china, ivory china, and progression china. In 1967, Noritake Imari Porcelain Manufacturing Co. and in 1968, Noritake Kyuto Co., Ltd. were established and took charge of the production of ivory, bone, and progression china respectively.

Noritake expanded its exports to include crystal glassware, stainless steel flatware, and melamineware in the early part of the 1960s. Besides the chinaware plants, Noritake now has a stainless steel flatware factory in Tsubame, which is located in the northern part of central Japan. The Atsugi plant is located near Tokyo and manufactures high crystal glassware, and the melamineware factory in Anjo, in the eastern side of Nagoya, is the biggest manufacturer of melamineware in Japan

In January 1970, by utilizing long experienced precision technology and also the technique of printing decals for chinaware and ceramics, Noritake decided to expand the manufacturing in the electronics field and started to manufacture electronics components and new ceramics products, such as vacuum fluorescent display tubes, thick-film printed circuit substrates, high brightness picture tubes, plasma display, ceramics for electronics components (molded parts substrates), new ceramics pipe, and dental ceramics. The electronics and new ceramics products grew rapidly and greatly contributed to the increase of the company business. As of the end of March 1999, this division became the largest division beyond the tabletop and abrasive grinding wheel divisions.

In 1972, Noritake established Noritake Lanka Porcelain (Pvt.) Ltd. in Sri Lanka, and in 1974, established Noritake Porcelana Mfg., Inc. in the Philippines. Both factories produce porcelain ware and are now the largest chinaware suppliers among the Noritake group.

Thus, Noritake is not only a chinaware manufacturer and exporter but also abrasive grinding wheels, electronics, and new ceramics parts manufacturer and exporter.

A Trip to the Noritake Company

Recently, I visited the Noritake Company headquarters in Nagoya, Japan. It was a most exciting event, and using some of my photos and those provided by Keishi Suzuki, I'd like to take readers on an armchair visit to the factory.

After taking the bullet train from Tokyo to Nagoya, it was a quick trip to the factory from the train station. My first view of the complex was a large building on the corner of the street. The original factory building soon came into view, and it was just like making a pilgrimage. This building is in remarkably good condition, and the company is hoping to eventually turn it into a much larger museum than they now have.

I toured the Welcome Center and a decorating studio that was located in the main building. The large vases and urns being decorated there were incredibly beautiful and most were very, very expensive. Only extremely qualified artists are allowed to work on these "museum quality" items. Showcases on the first floor contained beautiful figurines the company produces.

One of the most rewarding parts of the tour was viewing some of the original sketches for dinnerware patterns that an artist drew early in the twentieth century.

Although the museum is not huge in size it does contain some wonderful pieces of porcelain. The company is very proud of the items that were produced during the Nippon era (1891 – 1921) and with good reason.

Just before entering the museum, visitors encounter a large presentation piece that was made especially for the ribbon cutting ceremony when the museum was opened in 1979. In fact, the American ambassador to Japan cut the ribbon. This particular piece took three months to produce and most of that time was spent with the decorating.

An 1879 photo of the Morimura Brothers store in New York City hangs on a wall of the museum. There is also a case showing a model and sketch of one of the old kilns. On the top shelf the written oath of the founders is proudly displayed.

My personal favorite in the museum had to be the bound artist design sketchbooks. I was able to view several of them, and photos of a number of these pages are included in this book, thanks to the efforts of Keishi Suzuki. They are truly works of art as each is hand painted.

In 1914, the company manufactured its first dinner plate called Sedan, D1441. The backstamp is "Noritake, M in wreath, hand painted Nippon" and two of these plates are showcased in one of the cabinets.

Although collectors call early pieces of porcelain manufactured in Japan, Nippon, the company refers to their early porcelain pieces as old Noritake and that, of course, is what they are. The word "Nippon" was placed on items manufactured in Japan from 1891 to 1921, and although the majority was made by the Noritake Company, some pieces were manufactured by other companies in Japan. The two words are not synonymous: A beautiful scenic covered urn is featured in a display case and has a sign in front declaring that it is old Noritake.

Many items are featured in a multitude of display cases flanking the musuem's outer walls and also in the middle of the room. A number of cases also feature post-1921 items, but of course, my attention was focused on the Nippon era ones. The following photos show many of the showcases in the museum. The last photo is of Keishi Suzuki, my friend and host for this trip. He has been a great help to me with all the information he was able to share on the Noritake Company.

My first view was of this Noritake Co. building.

The original factory.

Welcome Center.

Decorating studio.

Showcases on first floor in model plant.

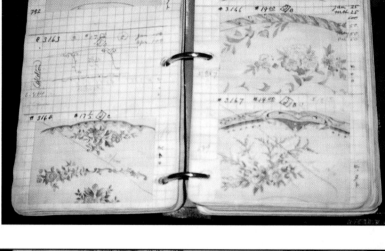

Entrance to museum.

This presentation piece was made especially for the ribbon cutting ceremony which opened the museum in 1979. The American ambassador to Japan cut the ribbon. This particular piece took three months to produce and most of that time was spent with the decorating.

Original sketch book and order book from 1897.

Sketch book pages for dinnerware found in the company's archives.

This 1879 photograph hangs on a wall of the musuem, picturing the Morimura Bros. store in New York City.

The written oath of founders.

The Noritake Company does not refer to the older items, such as these shown in cases, as Nippon but as old Noritake.

Top shelf: First dinner plate manufactured in the Noritake factory in 1914. It is pattern D1441 Sedan. The backstamp is "Noritake, M in wreath, hand painted Nippon." Bottom shelf: A duplicate of first plate.

Close-up of bottom shelf with model and sketch of old kiln.

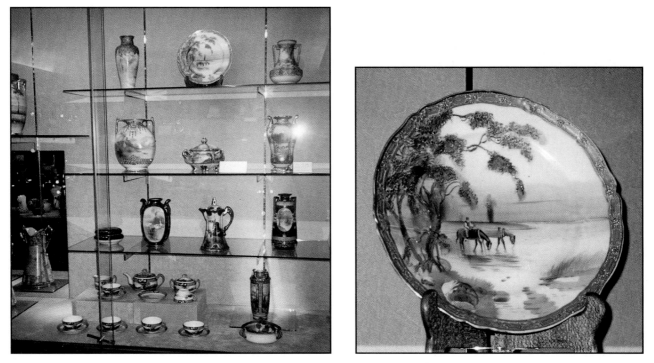

Left: Showcase filled with Nippon era pieces. Right: Close-up of top shelf item.

Showcase with close-up of large vase on bottom row.

Showcases filled with Nippon era pieces.

Showcase with close-up of tea set.

Showcases filled with Nippon era pieces.

Showcases filled with Nippon era pieces.

Nippon items found in glass showcases in middle of room.

Second row, middle: The cobalt and scenic vase with certificate was donated to the museum by this author.

Beautiful chocolate set on display.

Morimura dolls are on upper shelf.

Right: Nippon items found in showcase.

Showcase with close-up of items on bottom row.

Keishi Suzuki

Noritake Company Design Sketches and Salesman's Pages

In the *Collector's Encyclopedia of Nippon Porcelain, Fifth Series*, a number of wonderful old salesman's pages were featured, and in this volume, 72 design sketches from the archives of the Noritake Co. in Nagoya, Japan, are shown. Mr. Keishi Suzuki and the Noritake Co. provided these wonderful photos for readers of this book, and they are simply beautiful. I am indebted to both Keishi and the Noritake Co., Ltd. in Nagoya for sharing these works of art with the readers of this book.

Both salesmen and artists used this artwork on a daily basis. Each is hand painted, and since all hand-painted work varies slightly, we can assume that many of the finished items may have been just a little different than these original paintings.

Many of the design sketches owned by the Noritake Co. in Nagoya are found in bound books, and several are on display in glass cabinets at the Noritake Co. Museum in Nagoya, Japan.

Artists from the Noritake design studio in New York City created the patterns and designs, and then they were sent to Japan for artists to use as a guide when painting the various wares.

Both the salesman's pages and design sketches were most likely created in New York City. The salesman's page has three holes on the side so that it could be placed in a three-ring binder. Many of these pages even have penciled remarks on them indicating just how many and what types of items customers had ordered. The design sketches do not have holes on the side as they were bound in books.

According to Mr. Suzuki, there were eleven Noritake Co. salesmen in the United States who would have been in possession of the salesman's pages during this time period. Very few are now known to exist as they were probably thrown out much as we discard catalogs today. Each salesman's pages, however, is so highly prized that its price would be hundreds of dollars, most likely more expensive than the actual item it portrays. The design sketches have only been found in the company archives, and I know of no collector who has been able to purchase them.

Some collectors who own the salesman's pages enjoy finding the matching items and displaying the pieces together.

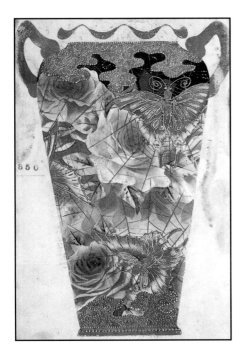

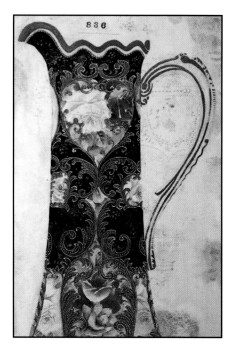

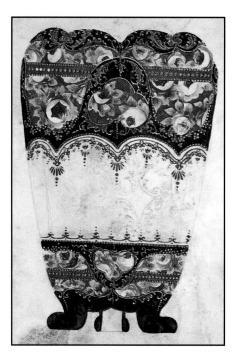

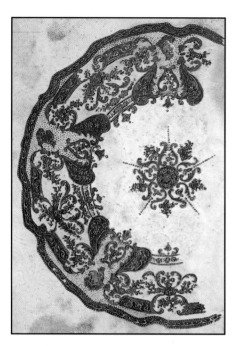

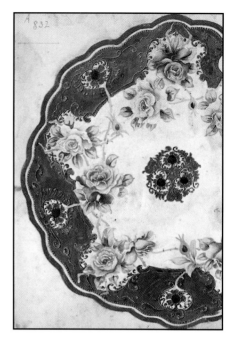

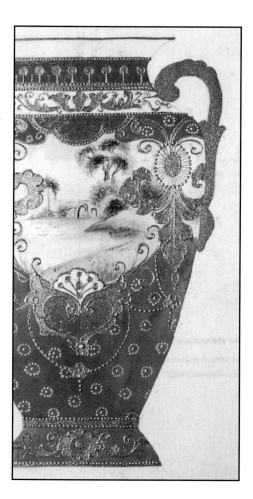

Kimonos Being Manufactured with Old Noritake Designs

Nippon enthusiasts will be thrilled to know that Japanese kimonos that have copies of several of the old Nippon era patterns as their designs are being manufactured.

Special permission from both the Noritake Co. and the kimono dress company has allowed us to print a portion of their brochure in this book. The kimono dress company's name is Nijoh Maruhachi Co., Limited, 1-2-3 Saganaka-dai, Kizu-cho, Sorakugun, Kyoto, Japan 619-02.

These particular kimonos are for weddings and are called Uchikake.

The kimonos are breathtakingly beautiful and are faithful reproductions of several of the old Noritake designs. Lucky is the bride who gets to wear one of them!

Keishi Suzuki from the Noritake Co. Ltd. in Nagoya, Japan, provided the brochures. He is a great resource for information and has been a tremendous help to me with my books.

I want to thank Keishi, the Noritake Co., Ltd., and the Nijoh Maruhachi Co. for sharing this information with readers of this book.

舞CURREN

スタイリング自由の舞カレン‥‥
　貴方だけの晴れのスタイルを見つけてください。

アールヌーボー薔薇

薔薇は、日本でも平安時代の歌に
いくつか詠まれています。その歴
史は西欧では古く、野薔薇だけで
はなく、園芸鑑賞種として様々な
花のバリエーションが生まれま
した。文様や絵画のモチーフとして、
アールヌーボーやアールデコの
様式美のなかに咲きほこる、まさ
に華の女王を、衣に咲かせました。

140-005CK

140-005YM

Mr. Ikuo Fukunaga, an employee of Morimura Shoji (Morimura Brothers in English) provided the following information.

Morimura Shoji is a worldwide import-export company. They currently import various kinds of aluminum and titanium products for aircraft from the United States, bauxite from Brazil, quartz from India, magnesium from Norway, whiskey malt from the United Kingdom, and so on. They also export fine ceramic products and car parts to many countries and distribute tabular alumina produced by Moralco exclusively as the sole agent in the domestic market.

Morimura Brothers (Morimura Gumi in Japanese), many years ago gathered a number of potters and craftsmen to produce various ceramics under the Morimura Gumi name. For example, the Kawahara factory in Tokyo, Ishida factory in Kyoto, Saigo factory in Nagoya, and so on were all producing works for Morimura Gumi.

At that time (from the 1890s to 1920s), there were excellent designers working at Morimura Brothers in New York such as Matsutaro Waki, Toranosuke Miyanaga, Yukio Takema, Tadao Waki, and Cyril W. Leigh, an Englishman. They drew very fascinating and very fashionable designs that would appeal to American customers.

Such designs were sent to Morimura Gumi in Tokyo. The people at Morimura Gumi took these designs to the Morimura Gumi factories and gave exact instructions to the potters and craftsmen who had never been in America or Europe. They took the steps necessary to ensure that the potters and craftsmen produced Morimura "fine" china.

At the beginning of the twentieth century, Morimura Gumi decided to centralize their operation in Nagoya and moved their various craftsmen to this location. In 1904, Morimura Gumi set up their own factory, Nippon Toki (now called Noritake Company) to produce the porcelain under their own brand

The leaders of Morimura Gumi in 1910. Back row, left to right: Kaisaku Morimura, second president of Morimura Gumi; Yasukata Murai, general manager of Morimura Bros., Inc.; Kazuchika Okura, the first president of Nippon Toki. Front row, left to right: Magobe Okura, general manager of Morimura Gumi; Ichitaro Morimura, the founder of Morimura Gumi; Saneyoshi Hirose, president of Morimura Bank.

name, Noritake China. Noritake is the name of the place where the factory was built.

The fine china fired in this period is referred to as "old Noritake" especially the "Nippon back-stamped porcelain." Morimura Gumi exported china of very high quality.

In the middle of the eighteenth century, Ichizaemon Morimura the First arrived in Edo (now called Tokyo) from Enshu (which means a place far away from Kyoto, the old capital of Japan). Edo was the capital of Japan in the Tokugawa era and was gradually becoming a prosperous city in the eighteenth century. The Morimura family began business at a place called Kyobashi near Ginza. Their first venture was to produce saddles and harnesses for horses.

Ichizaemon Morimura the Sixth, the hero of the Morimura Gumi story, succeeded to the family business, and it was his good fortune to be in the right place at the right time. The old Japan was about to give way to a new age of opportunity. An American naval office, Commodore Perry, created this new tide. Perry commanded an American fleet, the East India Squadron. In June 1853, the Perry squadron entered Edo Bay (now called Tokyo Bay). These ships, known as "Kuro Fune" in Japanese, and black ships in English, broke more than 200 years of national isolation. Commodore Perry demanded that Japan should be opened to international trade.

With this step, the floodgates were opened, and Japan was drawn out of isolationism. In 1854, Japan concluded a treaty with America that was called The Treaty of Peace and Amity between the United States of America and the Empire of Japan. This was the first treaty Japan concluded with a foreign country. In 1859, Japan opened three ports, Yokohama, Kobe, and Nagasaki to trade.

On July 4, 1859, American Independence Day, a consulate was set up at the Honkaku Temple in Kanagawa near Yokohama. A young American by the name of Eugene Miller Van Reed was one of the legation members. He was an assistant to the consul, General Dorr. Soon after this, Van Reed opened his own company in the Yokohama foreign settlement and began to live there.

Maybe, if Ichizaemon Morimura had not met this American, Van Reed, there would not have been a Morimura Gumi or any Nippon porcelain. Ichizaemon was a man of enterprise who went to Yokohama soon after the opening of this treaty port to seek a business opportunity. In a short time Ichizaemon became a trader who bought foreign goods at Yokohama to sell them in Edo. He visited Van Reed's firm many times. He heard from Van Reed about America and the world in general. This information motivated him to think about a business venture overseas.

Eugene Van Reed was born in 1835 in Reading, Pennsylvania. The date of his birth is not recorded on his gravestone at the Oak Hill Memorial Park, San Jose, California.

The reason why Van Reed came to Japan may be due to a chance meeting in his youth. In September 1850, the Japanese cargo ship *Sumiyoshi Maru* was wrecked in a storm on its way from Osaka to Edo. The ship drifted in the Pacific for more than 50 days. Seventeen sailors were eventually rescued by the American merchant ship *Oakland* and brought to San Francisco.

Eugene Van Reed (who was fifteen years old at this time) and his father had moved from Reading to San Francisco. There, Eugene Van Reed met one of the shipwrecked sailors, Hikozo Hamada, a Japanese boy who was two years younger than himself. He learned elementary Japanese from Hikozo and took an interest in Japan, an unknown country.

Fortunately, the Japanese boy Hikozo came across what is called a long-legged uncle or a patron by the name of Thunders, a banker from Baltimore. Thunders brought this boy to his house to educate him in Baltimore in 1853. Hikozo attended a mission school and was baptized as a Catholic. After this, he became known as Joseph Heco and was the first Japanese to be naturalized as an American citizen, in 1858.

Left: Eugene Miller Van Reed (1835 – 1873). Right: Hikozo Hamada/Joseph Heco (1837 – 1897).

In June 1858, Joseph Heco visited Reading to see Eugene Van Reed. Joseph Heco wrote in his autobiography *The Narrative of a Japanese*, "I was given a heart-warming welcome in Reading." It was a trip to say goodbye to Van Reed. In July, soon after this, Joseph left Baltimore and on September 26, 1858, set sail for Japan from San Francisco on board a surveying schooner, the *Fenimore Cooper*.

After Joseph Heco left America, Van Reed felt an even greater desire to see Japan for himself. Van Reed asked his friend, Jacob Knabb, who was the chief editor of *Berks and Schuylkill Journal*, a Reading newspaper, to appoint him as a correspondent for the newspaper. After getting Knabb's approval, Van Reed hurried back to San Francisco.

On February 2, 1859, he took passage on a clipper called the *Sea Serpent* from San Francisco. Margaret, Van Reed's younger sister, said in her later years, "My brother started for Japan being urged by the spirit of adventure." On April 6, Van Reed arrived in Hong Kong, where he wrote "California to Japan." This article appeared in the newspaper, *Berks and Schuylkill Journal* on June 25.

Ichizaemon Morimura, who learned various things about the foreign world, such as the state of affairs in America from Van Reed, persuaded his younger brother, Toyo, to enter the Keio Gijyuku University with the idea of making him proficient in English. Ichizaemon thought that English would be necessary if they were to begin a foreign trade venture.

In the spring of 1876, Ichizaemon and his younger brother, Toyo, established a small company, Morimura Gumi at their family store, Ginza, Tokyo. On March 10, Toyo went on board an American liner, the *Oceanic*, with four colleagues, who wished to learn American business under the supervision of Momotaro Sato, who had stayed many years in America. He had learned business at commercial schools and had already set up his own company on Front Street in Manhattan.

On April 10, 1876, the *Oceanic* group arrived in New York. After finishing a short course at the Eastman Business College in Poughkeepsie, New York, Toyo Morimura established a retail store named Hinode Shokai meaning "Rising Sun Firm" at 258 Sixth Street, New York City, in a partnership with Momotaro Sato and another colleague, each of whom invested $3,000.00.

Two years later in 1878, this partnership was dissolved and Toyo became independent. Hinode Shokai was reorganized and became Morimura Brothers. Morimura Gumi in Tokyo collected various Japanese goods, such as antiques, china, bronze, fans, dolls, and so on, and forwarded them to Hinode Shokai and Morimura Bros. These Japanese goods sold very well for good prices. Morimura Brothers in New York City began to get prosperous, and this situation continued until World War II.

The fine china line, a new business of Morimura Gumi and Morimura Brothers began in about 1887. Japan had a long tradition of producing fine quality

Van Reed riding his horse on the grounds of his house at No. 33 in the foreign settlement.

china, and Morimura Gumi enlisted the services of many factories and craftsmen around the country.

Noritake dinnerware of a pure white color produced by Nippon Toki was introduced in 1914, after a ten year trial-and-error period, with great success. From this point on Nippon Toki began to produce less and less hand-painted fine china.

By coincidence, this was the year that saw the outbreak of war in Europe. This prevented American merchants from importing bisque dolls from Europe, that were mainly produced in France and Germany. The American market ran short of stock, and this created a favorable situation for Morimura Gumi to establish a factory for producing bisque dolls in Nagoya.

As a first step, Morimura Gumi set up a ceramic research laboratory for the production of ceramic toys on the site of the Nippon Toki factory in March 1916. In 1917, Morimura Gumi established Nippon Gangu (Japan Toy) Co. with a capital of 200,000 yen and constructed a factory for making Morimura

bisque dolls at Sanbon Aze 1,616, Sakou-cho, Nishiku, Nagoya. Hirose Jikko was made president and Yamachi Torataro, general manager.

On this project, Morimura Gumi worked in concert with Frobel House, a playthings shop in Kanda, Tokyo, which still exists at Kanda Ogawa-cho 3-1, Chou-ku, Tokyo. Frobel House provided technical assistance and dispatched some personnel to Nippon Gangu. Morimura Brothers distributed the so-called Morimura bisque dolls in the American market.

However, World War I drew to a close in 1918, and the European producers returned to the American market. Although the quality of Morimura bisque dolls was on a par with that of European products, Morimura Brothers were forced to withdraw from the American market as they were unable to compete on price with the devaluation of European currencies. Nippon Gangu closed its door in 1921.

The business activities of Morimura Brothers in the United States had continued for 65 years until 1941, the beginning of World War II.

Dinner celebration in honor of the 40th anniversary of Morimura Brothers and the opening of their new building at No. 53-55-57 W. 23rd St., New York, February 9, 1917.

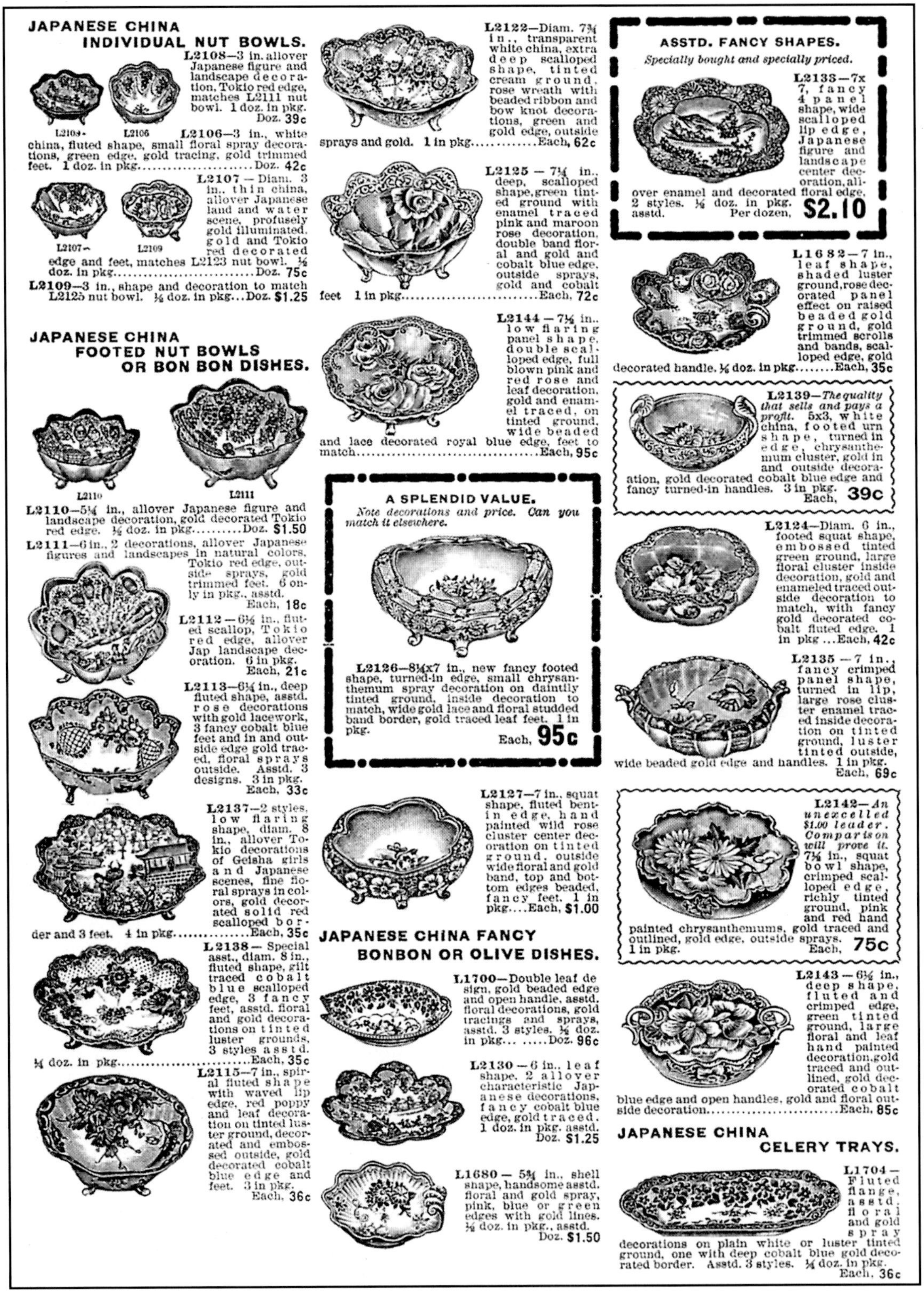

JAPANESE CHINA INDIVIDUAL NUT BOWLS.

L2108 L2106

L2108—3 in. allover Japanese figure and landscape decoration, Tokio red edge, matches L2111 nut bowl. 1 doz. in pkg. Doz. **39c**

L2106—3 in., white china, fluted shape, small floral spray decorations, green edge, gold tracing, gold trimmed feet. 1 doz. in pkg.......................Doz. **42c**

L2107 L2109

L2107—Diam. 3 in., thin china, allover Japanese land and water scene, profusely gold illuminated, gold and Tokio red decorated edge and feet, matches L2123 nut bowl. ½ doz. in pkg..........................Doz. **75c**

L2109—3 in., shape and decoration to match L2125 nut bowl. ½ doz. in pkg...Doz. **$1.25**

JAPANESE CHINA FOOTED NUT BOWLS OR BON BON DISHES.

L2110 L2111

L2110—5¼ in., allover Japanese figure and landscape decoration, gold decorated Tokio red edge. ½ doz. in pkg.........Doz. **$1.50**

L2111—6 in., 2 decorations, allover Japanese figures and landscapes in natural colors, Tokio red edge, outside sprays, gold trimmed feet. 6 only in pkg., asstd. Each, **18c**

L2112—6½ in., fluted scallop, Tokio red edge, allover Jap landscape decoration. 6 in pkg. Each, **21c**

L2113—6¼ in., deep fluted shape, asstd. rose decorations with gold lacework, 3 fancy cobalt blue feet and in and outside edge gold traced, floral sprays outside. Asstd. 3 designs. 3 in pkg. Each, **33c**

L2137—2 styles, low flaring shape, diam. 8 in., allover Tokio decorations of Geisha girls and Japanese scenes, fine floral sprays in colors, gold decorated solid red scalloped border and 3 feet. 4 in pkg...............Each, **35c**

L2138—Special asst., diam. 8 in., fluted shape, gilt traced cobalt blue scalloped edge, 3 fancy feet, asstd. floral and gold decorations on tinted luster grounds, 3 styles asstd. ¼ doz. in pkg..........................Each, **35c**

L2115—7 in., spiral fluted shape with waved lip edge, red poppy and leaf decoration on tinted luster ground, decorated and embossed outside, gold decorated cobalt blue edge and feet. 3 in pkg. Each, **36c**

L2122—Diam. 7¾ in., transparent white china, extra deep scalloped shape, tinted cream ground, rose wreath with beaded ribbon and bow knot decorations, green and gold edge, outside sprays and gold. 1 in pkg............Each, **62c**

L2125—7¼ in., deep, scalloped shape, green tinted ground with enamel traced pink and maroon rose decoration, double band floral and gold and cobalt blue edge, outside sprays, gold and cobalt feet 1 in pkg..........................Each, **72c**

L2144—7½ in., low flaring panel shape, double scalloped edge, full blown pink and red rose and leaf decoration, gold and enamel traced, on tinted ground, wide beaded and lace decorated royal blue edge, feet to match..................................Each, **95c**

A SPLENDID VALUE.

Note decorations and price. Can you match it elsewhere.

L2126—8¼x7 in., new fancy footed shape, turned-in edge, small chrysanthemum spray decoration on daintily tinted ground, inside decoration to match, wide gold lace and floral studded band border, gold traced leaf feet. 1 in pkg. Each, **95c**

L2127—7 in., squat shape, fluted bent-in edge, hand painted wild rose cluster center decoration on tinted ground, outside wide floral and gold band, top and bottom edges beaded, fancy feet. 1 in pkg....Each, **$1.00**

JAPANESE CHINA FANCY BONBON OR OLIVE DISHES.

L1700—Double leaf design, gold beaded edge and open handle, asstd. floral decorations, gold tracings and sprays, asstd. 3 styles. ½ doz. in pkg... .....Doz. **96c**

L2130—6 in., leaf shape, 2 allover characteristic Japanese decorations, fancy cobalt blue edge, gold traced. 1 doz. in pkg. asstd. Doz. **$1.25**

L1680—5¾ in., shell shape, handsome asstd. floral and gold spray, pink, blue or green edges with gold lines. ½ doz. in pkg., asstd. Doz. **$1.50**

ASSTD. FANCY SHAPES.

Specially bought and specially priced.

L2133—7x7, fancy 4 panel shape, wide scalloped lip edge, Japanese figure and landscape center decoration, allover enamel and decorated floral edge, 2 styles. ½ doz. in pkg. asstd. Per dozen, **$2.10**

L1682—7 in., leaf shape, shaded luster ground, rose decorated panel effect on raised beaded gold ground, gold trimmed scrolls and bands, scalloped edge, gold decorated handle. ½ doz. in pkg........Each, **35c**

L2139—*The quality that sells and pays a profit.* 5x3, white china, footed urn shape, turned in edge, chrysanthemum cluster, gold in and outside decoration, gold decorated cobalt blue edge and fancy turned-in handles. 3 in pkg. Each, **39c**

L2124—Diam. 6 in., footed squat shape, embossed tinted green ground, large floral cluster inside decoration, gold and enameled traced outside decoration to match, with fancy gold decorated cobalt fluted edge. 1 in pkg ...Each, **42c**

L2135—7 in., fancy crimped panel shape, turned in lip, large rose cluster enamel traced inside decoration on tinted ground, luster tinted outside, wide beaded gold edge and handles. 1 in pkg. Each, **69c**

L2142—*An unexcelled $1.00 leader. Comparison will prove it.* 7½ in., squat bowl shape, crimped scalloped edge, richly tinted ground, pink and red hand painted chrysanthemums, gold traced and outlined, gold edge, outside sprays. 1 in pkg. Each, **75c**

L2143—6½ in., deep shape, fluted and crimped edge, green tinted ground, large floral and leaf hand painted decoration, gold traced and outlined, gold decorated cobalt blue edge and open handles, gold and floral outside decoration..........................Each, **85c**

JAPANESE CHINA CELERY TRAYS.

L1704—Fluted flange, asstd. floral and gold spray decorations on plain white or luster tinted ground, one with deep cobalt blue gold decorated border. Asstd. 3 styles. ¼ doz. in pkg. Each, **36c**

Butler Bros. Catalog, 1907.

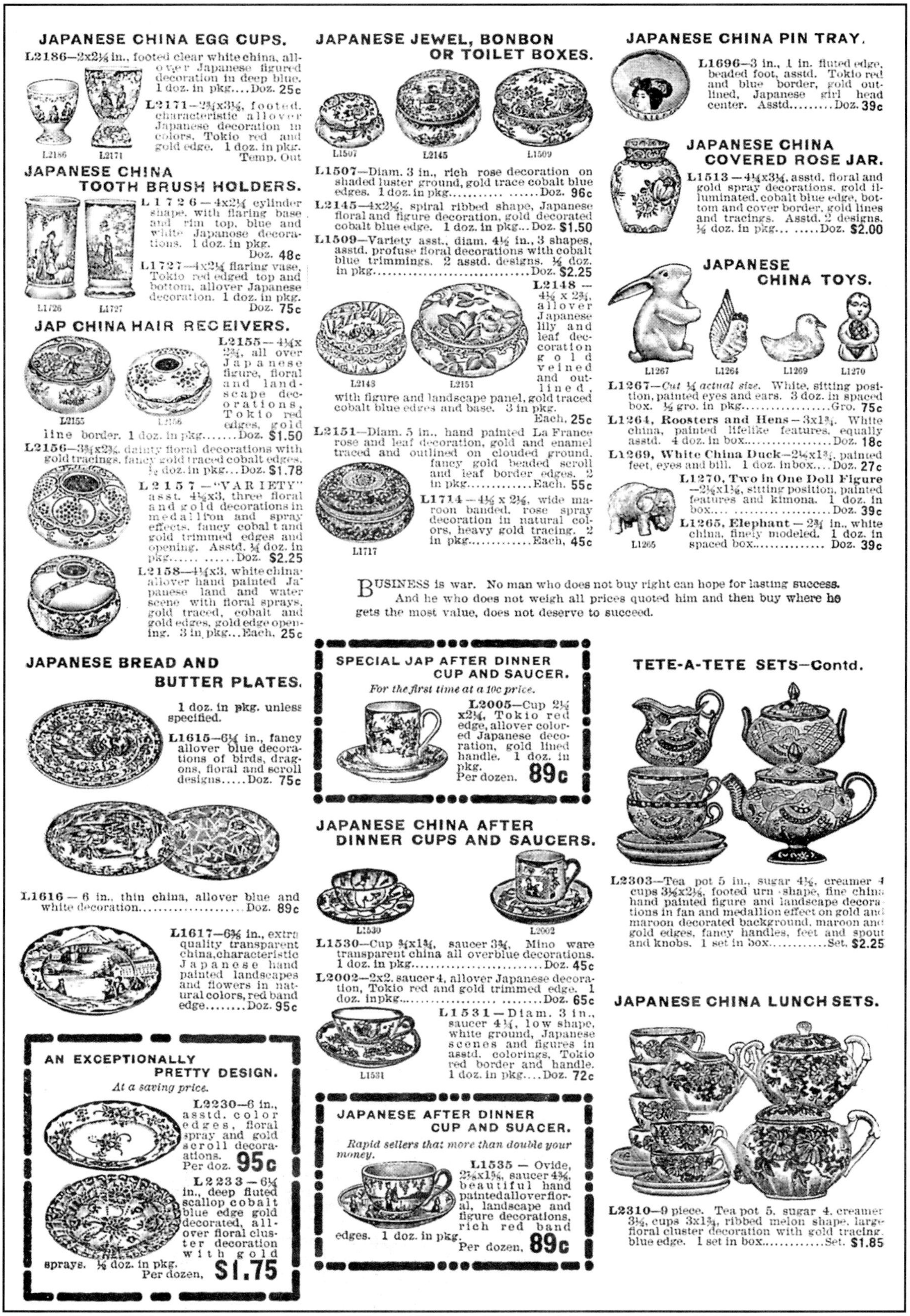

JAPANESE CHINA EGG CUPS.

L2186—2x2⅛ in., footed clear white china, allover Japanese figured decoration in deep blue. 1 doz. in pkg....Doz. 25c

L2171—2¾x3¼, footed. characteristic allover Japanese decoration in colors. Tokio red and gold edge. 1 doz. in pkg. Temp. Out

L2186 L2171

JAPANESE CHINA TOOTH BRUSH HOLDERS.

L1726—4x2¼ cylinder shape, with flaring base and rim top, blue and white Japanose decorations. 1 doz. in pkg. Doz. 48c

L1727—4x2¼ flaring vase, Tokio red edged top and bottom, allover Japanese decoration. 1 doz. in pkg. Doz. 75c

L1726 L1727

JAP CHINA HAIR RECEIVERS.

L2155—4¼x2¾, all over Japanese figure, floral and landscape decorations, Tokio red edges, gold line border. 1 doz. in pkg.......Doz. $1.50

L2155 L2156

L2156—3¾x2¾, dainty floral decorations with gold tracings, fancy gold traced cobalt edges. ½ doz. in pkg...Doz. $1.78

L2157—"VARIETY" asst. 4½x3, three floral and gold decorations in medallion and spray effects, fancy cobalt and gold trimmed edges and opening. Asstd. ¼ doz. in pkg...... ......Doz. $2.25

L2158—4¼x3, white china allover hand painted Japanese land and water scene with floral sprays, gold traced, cobalt and gold edges, gold edge opening. 3 in pkg...Each. 25c

JAPANESE JEWEL, BONBON OR TOILET BOXES.

L1507 L2145 L1509

L1507—Diam. 3 in., rich rose decoration on shaded luster ground, gold trace cobalt blue edges. 1 doz. in pkg.......... ......Doz. 96c

L2145—4x2½, spiral ribbed shape, Japanese floral and figure decoration, gold decorated cobalt blue edge. 1 doz. in pkg...Doz. $1.50

L1509—Variety asst., diam. 4½ in., 3 shapes, asstd. profuse floral decorations with cobalt blue trimmings. 2 asstd. designs. ⅙ doz. in pkg............................Doz. $2.25

L2148—4½ x 2¾, allover Japanese lily and leaf decoration gold veined and outlined, with figure and landscape panel, gold traced cobalt blue edges and base. 3 in pkg. Each. 25c

L2148 L2151

L2151—Diam. 5 in., hand painted La France rose and leaf decoration, gold and enamel traced and outlined on clouded ground, fancy gold beaded scroll and leaf border edges. 2 in pkg............Each. 55c

L1714—4½ x 2½, wide maroon banded, rose spray decoration in natural colors, heavy gold tracing. 2 in pkg............Each, 45c

L1717

JAPANESE CHINA PIN TRAY.

L1696—3 in., 1 in. fluted edge, beaded foot, asstd. Tokio red and blue border, gold outlined, Japanese girl head center. Asstd.........Doz. 39c

JAPANESE CHINA COVERED ROSE JAR.

L1513—4¾x3¼, asstd. floral and gold spray decorations, gold illuminated, cobalt blue edge, bottom and cover border, gold lines and tracings. Asstd. 2 designs. ⅙ doz. in pkg... .....Doz. $2.00

JAPANESE CHINA TOYS.

L1267 L1264 L1269 L1270

L1267—*Cut ¼ actual size.* White, sitting position, painted eyes and ears. 3 doz. in spaced box. ½ gro. in pkg.................Gro. 75c

L1264, Roosters and Hens—3x1¾. White china, painted lifelike features, equally asstd. 4 doz. in box................Doz. 18c

L1269, White China Duck—2⅛x1¾, painted feet, eyes and bill. 1 doz. in box....Doz. 27c

L1270, Two in One Doll Figure—2⅛x1⅛, sitting position, painted features and kimona. 1 doz. in box.... ....Doz. 39c

L1265, Elephant—2¾ in., white china, finely modeled. 1 doz. in spaced box.............. Doz. 39c

L1265

BUSINESS is war. No man who does not buy right can hope for lasting success. And he who does not weigh all prices quoted him and then buy where he gets the most value, does not deserve to succeed.

JAPANESE BREAD AND BUTTER PLATES.

1 doz. in pkg. unless specified.

L1615—6¼ in., fancy allover blue decorations of birds, dragons, floral and scroll designs.....Doz. 75c

L1616—6 in., thin china, allover blue and white decoration....................Doz. 89c

L1617—6⅜ in., extra quality transparent china, characteristic Japanese hand painted landscapes and flowers in natural colors, red band edge........Doz. 95c

AN EXCEPTIONALLY PRETTY DESIGN.

At a saving price.

L2230—6 in., asstd. color edges, floral spray and gold scroll decorations. Per doz. 95c

L2233—6¼ in., deep fluted scallop cobalt blue edge gold decorated, allover floral cluster decoration with gold sprays. ⅙ doz. in pkg. Per dozen, $1.75

SPECIAL JAP AFTER DINNER CUP AND SAUCER.

For the first time at a 10c price.

L2005—Cup 2⅛x2¼, Tokio red edge, allover colored Japanese decoration, gold lined handle. 1 doz. in pkg. Per dozen. 89c

JAPANESE CHINA AFTER DINNER CUPS AND SAUCERS.

L1530 L2002

L1530—Cup ¾x1¾, saucer 3¾, Mino ware transparent china all overblue decorations. 1 doz. in pkg.........................Doz. 45c

L2002—2x2, saucer 4, allover Japanese decoration, Tokio red and gold trimmed edge. 1 doz. inpkg.................. ....Doz. 65c

L1531—Diam. 3 in., saucer 4¼, low shape, white ground, Japanese scenes and figures in asstd. colorings, Tokio red border and handle. 1 doz. in pkg....Doz. 72c

L1531

JAPANESE AFTER DINNER CUP AND SUACER.

Rapid sellers that more than double your money.

L1535—Ovide, 2⅜x1⅝, saucer 4⅜, beautiful hand painted allover floral, landscape and figure decorations, rich red band edges. 1 doz. in pkg. Per dozen, 89c

TETE-A-TETE SETS—Contd.

L2303—Tea pot 5 in., sugar 4½, creamer 4 cups 3⅛x2⅛, footed urn shape, fine china hand painted figure and landscape decorations in fan and medallion effect on gold and maroon decorated background, maroon and gold edges, fancy handles, feet and spout and knobs. 1 set in box...........Set. $2.25

JAPANESE CHINA LUNCH SETS.

L2310—9 piece. Tea pot 5. sugar 4. creamer 3½, cups 3x1¾, ribbed melon shape, large floral cluster decoration with gold tracing, blue edge. 1 set in box............Set. $1.85

Butler Bros. Catalog, 1907.

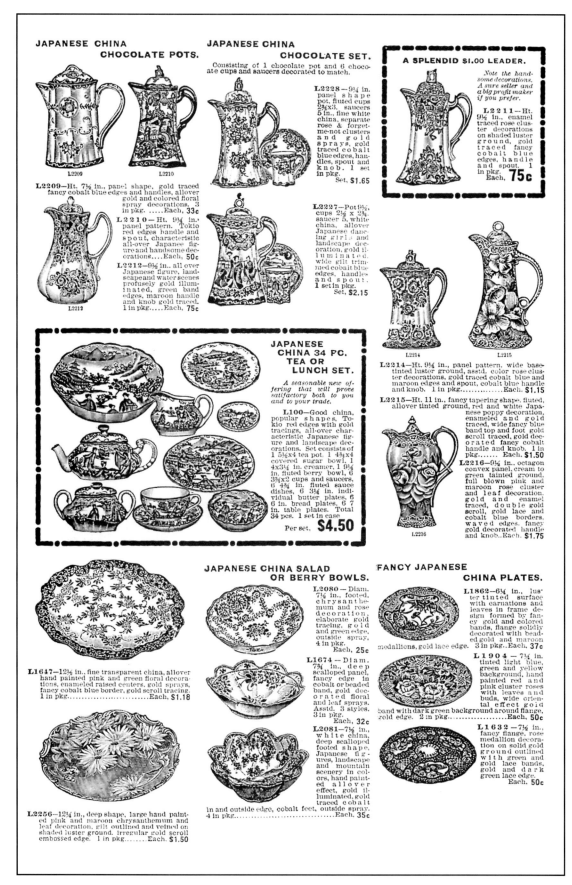

JAPANESE CHINA CHOCOLATE POTS.

L2209—Ht. 7½ in., panel shape, gold traced fancy cobalt blue edges and handles, allover gold and colored floral spray decorations. 3 in pkg. .....Each, 33c

L2210—Ht. 9¼ in., panel pattern. Tokio red edges handle and spout, characteristic all-over Japanee figure and handsome decorations....Each, 50c

L2212—9½ in., all over Japanese figure, landscape and water scenes profusely gold illuminated, green band edges, maroon handle and knob gold traced. 1 in pkg.....Each, 75c

JAPANESE CHINA CHOCOLATE SET.

Consisting of 1 chocolate pot and 6 chocolate cups and saucers decorated to match.

L2228—9¼ in. panel shape, fluted cups 2¾x3, saucers 5 in., fine white china, separate rose & forget-me-not clusters and gold sprays, gold traced cobalt blue edges, handles, spout and knob. 1 set in pkg. Set, $1.65

L2227—Pot 9½, cups 2½ x 2¾, saucer 5, white china, allover Japanese dancing girls and landscape decoration, gold illuminated, wide gilt trimmed cobalt blue edges, handles and spout. 1 set in pkg. Set, $2.15

L2214—Ht. 9¼ in., panel pattern, wide base tinted luster ground, asstd. color rose cluster decorations, gold traced cobalt blue and maroon edges and spout, cobalt blue handle and knob. 1 in pkg..............Each. $1.15

L2215—Ht. 11 in., fancy tapering shape, fluted, allover tinted ground, red and white Japanese poppy decoration, enameled and gold traced, wide fancy blue band top and foot gold scroll traced, gold decorated fancy cobalt handle and knob. 1 in pkg....... Each. $1.50

L2216—9½ in., octagon convex panel, cream to green tainted ground, full blown pink and maroon rose cluster and leaf decoration, gold and enamel traced, double gold scroll, gold lace and cobalt blue borders, waved edges, fancy gold decorated handle and knob..Each. $1.75

JAPANESE CHINA 34 PC. TEA OR LUNCH SET.

A seasonable new offering that will prove satifactory both to you and to your trade.

L100—Good china, popular shapes, Tokio red edges with gold tracings, all-over characteristic Japanese figure and landscape decorations. Set consists of 1 5¼x4 tea pot, 1 4¾x4 covered sugar bowl, 1 4x3¼ in. creamer, 1 9¼ in. fluted berry bowl, 6 3¾x2 cups and saucers, 6 4¾ in. fluted sauce dishes, 6 3¼ in. individual butter plates, 6 6 in. bread plates, 6 7 in. table plates. Total 34 pcs. 1 set in case Per set. $4.50

JAPANESE CHINA SALAD OR BERRY BOWLS.

L2080—Diam. 7½ in., footed, chrysanthemum and rose decoration, elaborate gold tracing, gold and green edge, outside spray, 4 in pkg. Each, 25c

L1674—Diam. 7¾ in., deep scalloped panel, fancy edge in cobalt or beaded band, gold decorated floral and leaf sprays. Asstd. 3 styles. 3 in pkg. Each, 32c

L2081—7½ in., white china, deep scalloped footed shape, Japanese figures, landscape and mountain scenery in colors, hand painted allover effect, gold illuminated, gold traced cobalt in and outside edge, cobalt feet, outside spray. 4 in pkg.................................Each, 35c

L1647—12½ in., fine transparent china, allover hand painted pink and green floral decorations, enameled raised centers, gold sprays, fancy cobalt blue border, gold scroll tracing. 1 in pkg...........................Each, $1.18

L2256—12¼ in., deep shape, large hand painted pink and maroon chrysanthemum and leaf decoration, gilt outlined and veined on shaded luster ground, irregular gold scroll embossed edge. 1 in pkg....... Each. $1.50

FANCY JAPANESE CHINA PLATES.

L1862—6¼ in., luster tinted surface with carnations and leaves in frame design formed by fancy gold and colored bands, flange solidly decorated with beaded gold and maroon medallions, gold lace edge. 3 in pkg..Each. 37c

L1904—7¼ in. tinted light blue, green and yellow background, hand painted red and pink cluster roses with leaves and buds, wide oriental effect gold band with dark green background around flange, gold edge. 2 in pkg...................Each. 50c

L1632—7½ in., fancy flange, rose medallion decoration on solid gold ground outlined with green and gold lace bands, gold and dark green lace edge. Each. 50c

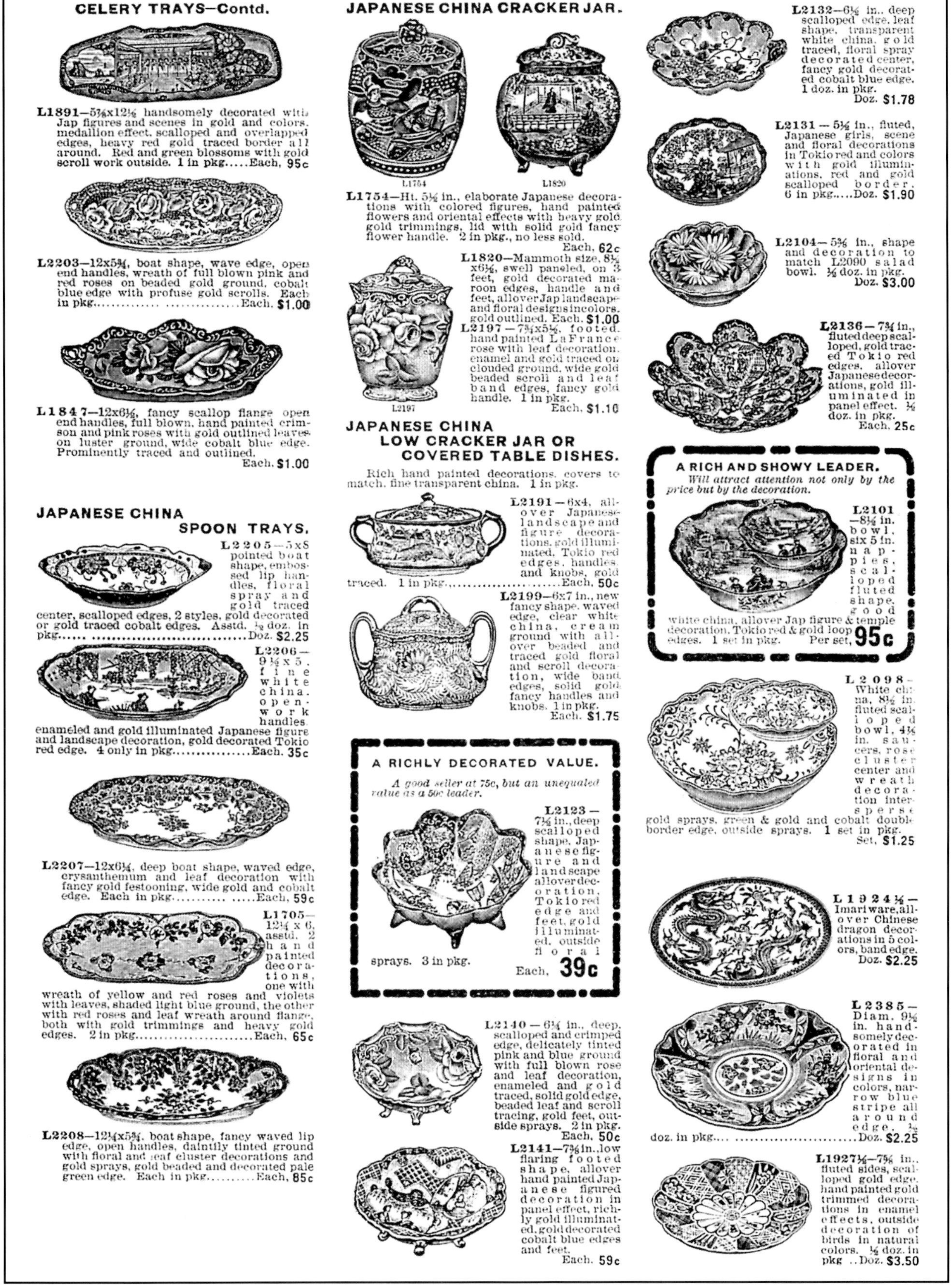

CELERY TRAYS—Contd.

L1891—5⅞x12½ handsomely decorated with Jap figures and scenes in gold and colors, medallion effect, scalloped and overlapped edges, heavy red gold traced border all around. Red and green blossoms with gold scroll work outside. 1 in pkg.....Each, 95c

L2203—12x5¾, boat shape, wave edge, open end handles, wreath of full blown pink and red roses on beaded gold ground, cobalt blue edge with profuse gold scrolls. Each in pkg..........................Each, $1.00

L1847—12x6½, fancy scallop flange open end handles, full blown, hand painted crimson and pink roses with gold outlined leaves on luster ground, wide cobalt blue edge. Prominently traced and outlined. Each, $1.00

JAPANESE CHINA SPOON TRAYS.

L2205—5x8 pointed boat shape, embossed lip handles, floral spray and gold traced center, scalloped edges, 2 styles, gold decorated or gold traced cobalt edges. Asstd. ½ doz. in pkg..................................Doz. $2.25

L2206—9½x5, fine white china, open-work handles enameled and gold illuminated Japanese figure and landscape decoration, gold decorated Tokio red edge. 4 only in pkg...............Each, 35c

L2207—12x6¼, deep boat shape, waved edge, crysanthemum and leaf decoration with fancy gold festooning, wide gold and cobalt edge. Each in pkg...............Each, 59c

L1705—12¼ x 6, asstd. 2 hand painted decorations, one with wreath of yellow and red roses and violets with leaves, shaded light blue ground, the other with red roses and leaf wreath around flange, both with gold trimmings and heavy gold edges. 2 in pkg..........................Each, 65c

L2208—12¼x5¾, boat shape, fancy waved lip edge, open handles, daintily tinted ground with floral and leaf cluster decorations and gold sprays, gold beaded and decorated pale green edge. Each in pkg..........Each, 85c

JAPANESE CHINA CRACKER JAR.

L1754 L1820

L1754—Ht. 5½ in., elaborate Japanese decorations with colored figures, hand painted flowers and oriental effects with heavy gold, gold trimmings, lid with solid gold fancy flower handle. 2 in pkg., no less sold. Each, 62c

L1820—Mammoth size, 8½ x6½, swell paneled, on 3 feet, gold decorated maroon edges, handle and feet, allover Jap landscape and floral designs in colors, gold outlined. Each, $1.00

L2197—7¾x5½, footed, hand painted La France rose with leaf decoration, enamel and gold traced on clouded ground, wide gold beaded scroll and leaf band edges, fancy gold handle. 1 in pkg. Each, $1.10

L2197

JAPANESE CHINA LOW CRACKER JAR OR COVERED TABLE DISHES.

Rich hand painted decorations, covers to match, fine transparent china. 1 in pkg.

L2191—6x4, allover Japanese landscape and figure decorations, gold illuminated, Tokio red edges, handles and knobs, gold traced. 1 in pkg..........................Each, 50c

L2199—6x7 in., new fancy shape, waved edge, clear white china, cream ground with allover beaded and traced gold floral and scroll decoration, wide band edges, solid gold fancy handles and knobs. 1 in pkg. Each, $1.75

A RICHLY DECORATED VALUE.

A good seller at 75c, but an unequaled value as a 50c leader.

L2123—7½ in., deep scalloped shape, Japanese figure and landscape allover decoration, Tokio red edge and feet, gold illuminated, outside floral sprays. 3 in pkg. Each, 39c

L2140—6¼ in., deep, scalloped and crimped edge, delicately tinted pink and blue ground with full blown rose and leaf decoration, enameled and gold traced, solid gold edge, beaded leaf and scroll tracing, gold feet, outside sprays. 2 in pkg. Each, 50c

L2141—7⅝ in., low flaring footed shape, allover hand painted Japanese figured decoration in panel effect, richly gold illuminated, gold decorated cobalt blue edges and feet. Each, 59c

L2132—6½ in., deep scalloped edge, leaf shape, transparent white china, gold traced, floral spray decorated center, fancy gold decorated cobalt blue edge. 1 doz. in pkg. Doz. $1.78

L2131—5½ in., fluted, Japanese girls, scene and floral decorations in Tokio red and colors with gold illuminations, red and gold scalloped border. 6 in pkg.....Doz. $1.90

L2104—5⅝ in., shape and decoration to match L2090 salad bowl. ½ doz. in pkg. Doz. $3.00

L2136—7¾ in., fluted deep scalloped, gold traced Tokio red edges, allover Japanese decorations, gold illuminated in panel effect. ½ doz. in pkg. Each, 25c

A RICH AND SHOWY LEADER.

Will attract attention not only by the price but by the decoration.

L2101—8½ in. bowl, six 5 in. nappies, scalloped fluted shape, good white china, allover Jap figure & temple decoration, Tokio red & gold loop edges. 1 set in pkg. Per set, 95c

L2098—White china, 8½ in. fluted scalloped bowl, 4½ in. saucers, rose cluster center and wreath decoration interspersed gold sprays, green & gold and cobalt double border edge, outside sprays. 1 set in pkg. Set, $1.25

L1924½—Imari ware, allover Chinese dragon decorations in 5 colors, band edge. Doz. $2.25

L2385—Diam. 9½ in. handsomely decorated in floral and oriental designs in colors, narrow blue stripe all around edge. ½ doz. in pkg.............................Doz. $2.25

L1927½—7⅝ in., fluted sides, scalloped gold edge, hand painted gold trimmed decorations in enamel effects, outside decoration of birds in natural colors. ½ doz. in pkg ..Doz. $3.50

Butler Bros. Catalog, 1907.

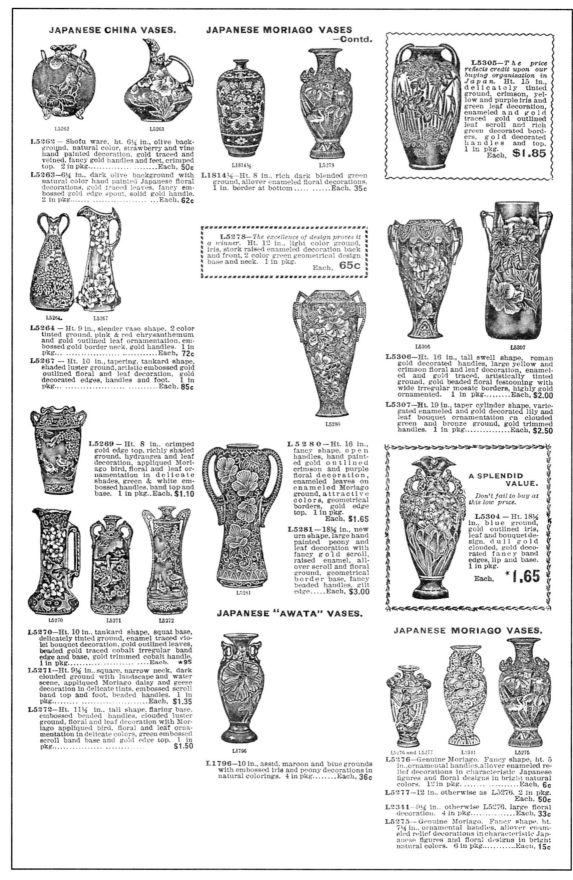

Butler Bros. Catalog, 1908.

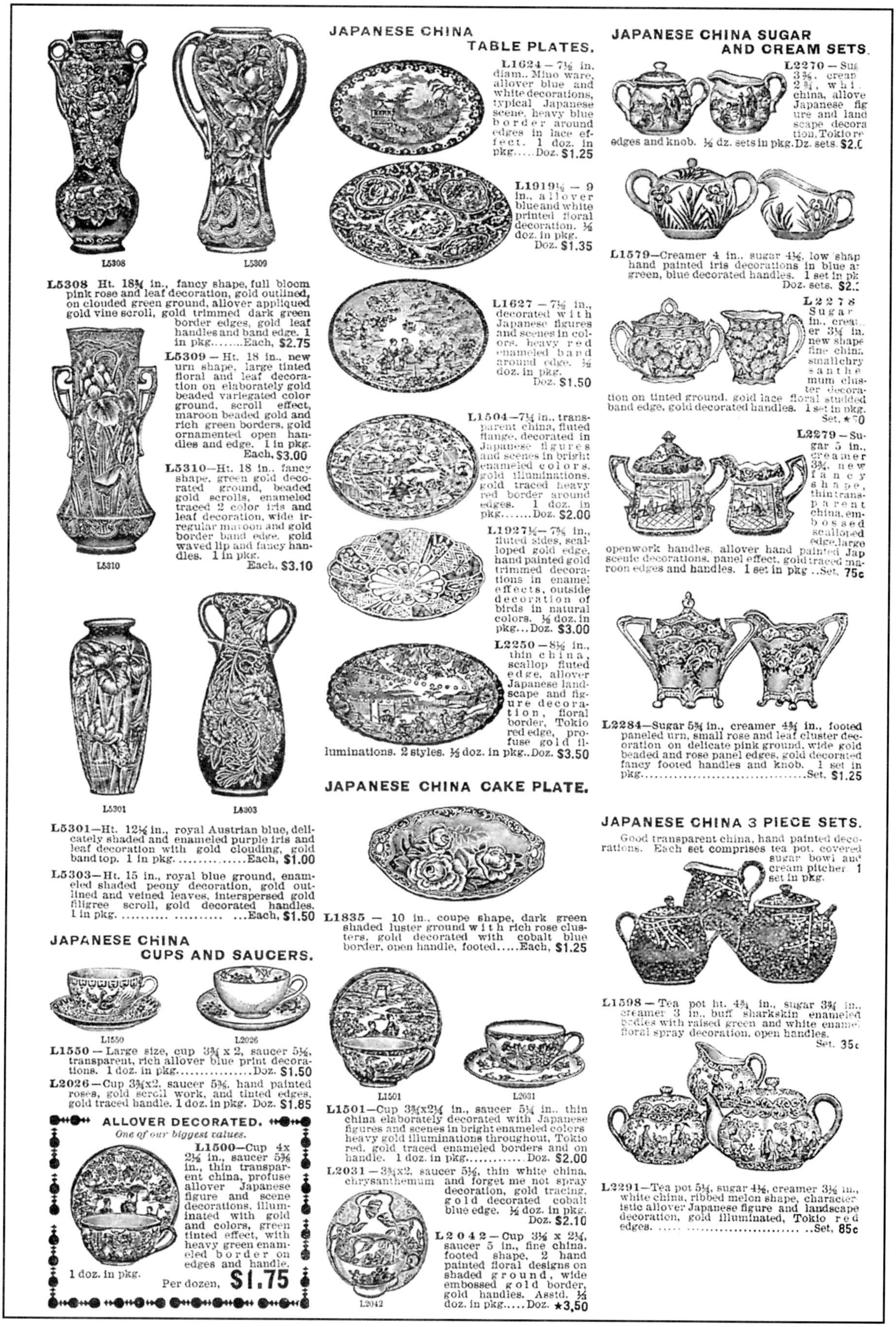

L5308 L5309

L5308 Ht. 18¾ in., fancy shape, full bloom pink rose and leaf decoration, gold outlined, on clouded green ground, allover appliqued gold vine scroll, gold trimmed dark green border edges, gold leaf handles and band edge. 1 in pkg........Each, $2.75

L5309—Ht. 18 in., new urn shape, large tinted floral and leaf decoration on elaborately gold beaded variegated color ground, scroll effect, maroon beaded gold and rich green borders, gold ornamented open handles and edge. 1 in pkg. Each, $3.00

L5310—Ht. 18 in., fancy shape, green gold decorated ground, beaded gold scrolls, enameled traced 2 color iris and leaf decoration, wide irregular maroon and gold border band edge, gold waved lip and fancy handles. 1 in pkg. Each, $3.10

L5310

L5301 L5303

L5301—Ht. 12⅛ in., royal Austrian blue, delicately shaded and enameled purple iris and leaf decoration with gold clouding, gold band top. 1 in pkg. ....Each, $1.00

L5303—Ht. 15 in., royal blue ground, enameled shaded peony decoration, gold outlined and veined leaves, interspersed gold filigree scroll, gold decorated handles. 1 in pkg. ....Each, $1.50

JAPANESE CHINA CUPS AND SAUCERS.

L1550 L2026

L1550—Large size, cup 3¾ x 2, saucer 5½, transparent, rich allover blue print decorations. 1 doz. in pkg................Doz. $1.50

L2026—Cup 3¾x2, saucer 5⅝, hand painted roses, gold scroll work, and tinted edges, gold traced handle. 1 doz. in pkg. Doz. $1.85

ALLOVER DECORATED.

One of our biggest values.

L1500—Cup 4x 2⅛ in., saucer 5⅝ in., thin transparent china, profuse allover Japanese figure and scene decorations, illuminated with gold and colors, green tinted effect, with heavy green enameled border on edges and handle.

1 doz. in pkg. Per dozen, $1.75

JAPANESE CHINA TABLE PLATES.

L1624—7½ in. diam.. Mino ware, allover blue and white decorations, typical Japanese scene, heavy blue border around edges in lace effect. 1 doz. in pkg.....Doz. $1.25

L1919½—9 in., allover blue and white printed floral decoration. ½ doz. in pkg. Doz. $1.35

L1627—7½ in., decorated with Japanese figures and scenes in colors, heavy red enameled band around edge. ½ doz. in pkg. Doz. $1.50

L1504—7¼ in., transparent china, fluted flange, decorated in Japanese figures and scenes in bright enameled colors, gold illuminations, gold traced heavy red border around edges. 1 doz. in pkg.......Doz. $2.00

L1927½—7⅝ in., fluted sides, scalloped gold edge, hand painted gold trimmed decorations in enamel effects, outside decoration of birds in natural colors. ½ doz. in pkg...Doz. $3.00

L2250—8⅛ in., thin china, scallop fluted edge, allover Japanese landscape and figure decoration, floral border, Tokio red edge, profuse gold illuminations. 2 styles. ½ doz. in pkg..Doz. $3.50

JAPANESE CHINA CAKE PLATE.

L1835 — 10 in., coupe shape, dark green shaded luster ground with rich rose clusters, gold decorated with cobalt blue border, open handle, footed.....Each, $1.25

L1501 L2031

L1501—Cup 3¾x2¼ in., saucer 5¼ in.. thin china elaborately decorated with Japanese figures and scenes in bright enameled colors heavy gold illuminations throughout, Tokio red, gold traced enameled borders and on handle. 1 doz. in pkg............Doz. $2.00

L2031—3¾x2, saucer 5½, thin white china, chrysanthemum and forget me not spray decoration, gold tracing, gold decorated cobalt blue edge. ½ doz. in pkg. Doz. $2.10

L2042—Cup 3⅛ x 2¼, saucer 5 in., fine china, footed shape, 2 hand painted floral designs on shaded ground, wide embossed gold border, gold handles. Asstd. ⅓ doz. in pkg.....Doz. ★3,50

L2042

JAPANESE CHINA SUGAR AND CREAM SETS.

L2270—Sug 3⅝, crean 2¾, whi china, allove Japanese fig ure and land scape decora tion, Tokio re edges and knob. ½ dz. sets in pkg. Dz. sets. $2.(

L1579—Creamer 4 in., sugar 4½, low shap hand painted iris decorations in blue a green, blue decorated handles. 1 set in pk Doz. sets. $2.:

L2278 Sugar in., crea er 3¼ in. new shape fine chin: small chrysanthemum cluster decoration on tinted ground, gold lace floral studded band edge, gold decorated handles. 1 set in pkg. Set, ★50

L2279—Sugar 5 in., creamer 3¾, new fancy shape, thin transparent china, embossed scalloped edge, large openwork handles, allover hand painted Jap scenic decorations, panel effect, gold traced maroon edges and handles. 1 set in pkg ..Set, 75c

L2284—Sugar 5¾ in., creamer 4¾ in., footed paneled urn, small rose and leaf cluster decoration on delicate pink ground, wide gold beaded and rose panel edges, gold decorated fancy footed handles and knob. 1 set in pkg.................................Set, $1.25

JAPANESE CHINA 3 PIECE SETS.

Good transparent china, hand painted decorations. Each set comprises tea pot, covered sugar bowl and cream pitcher 1 set in pkg.

L1598—Tea pot ht. 4¾ in., sugar 3¾ in., creamer 3 in., buff sharkskin enameled bodies with raised green and white enamel floral spray decoration, open handles. Set, 35c

L2291—Tea pot 5¼, sugar 4½, creamer 3½ in., white china, ribbed melon shape, characteristic allover Japanese figure and landscape decoration, gold illuminated, Tokio red edges. ....Set, 85c

Butler Bros. Catalog, 1908.

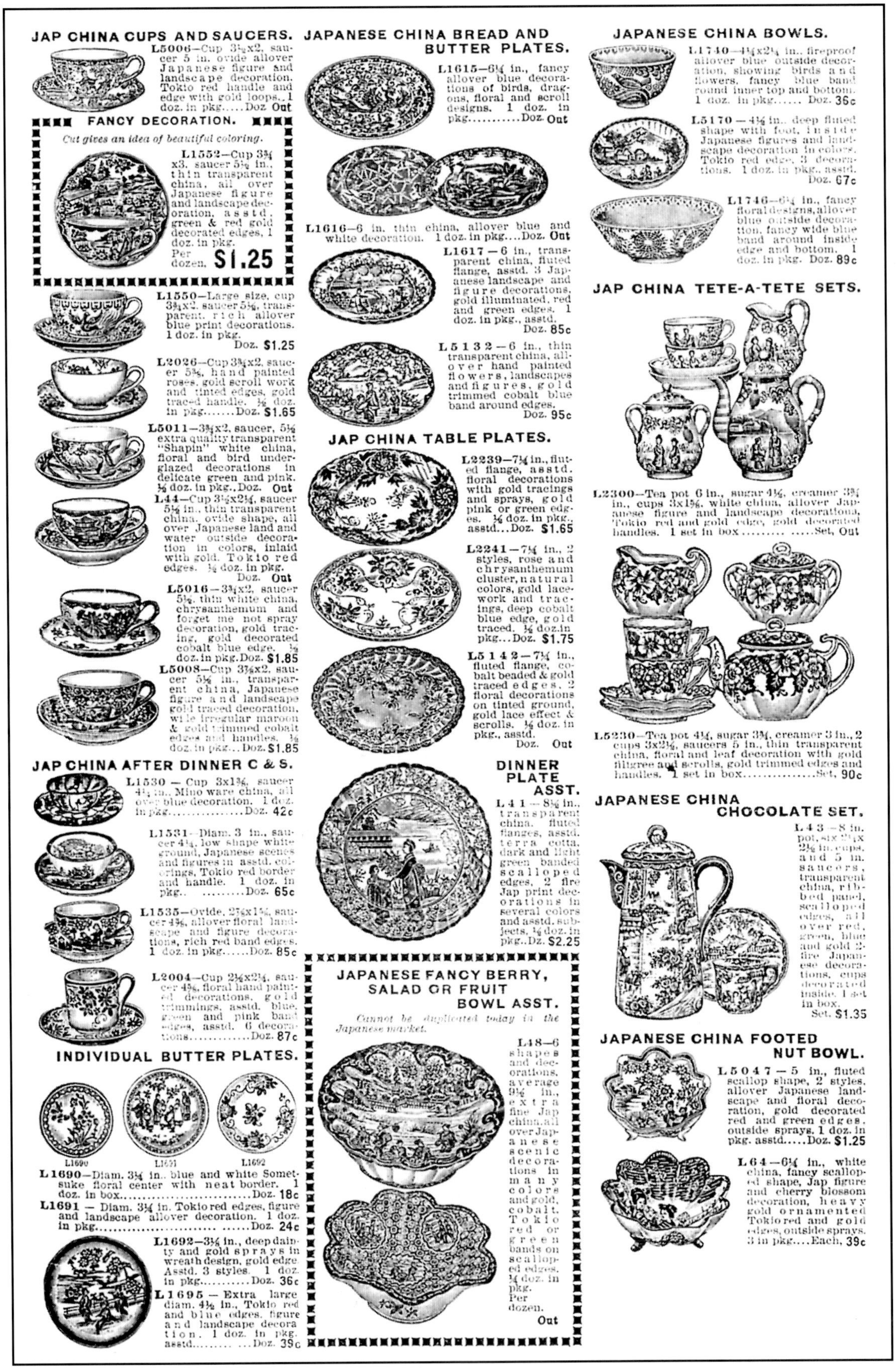

JAP CHINA CUPS AND SAUCERS.

L5006—Cup 3½x2, saucer 5 in. ovide allover Japanese figure and landscape decoration. Tokio red handle and edge with gold loops. 1 doz. in pkg.....Doz Out

FANCY DECORATION.

Cut gives an idea of beautiful coloring.

L1552—Cup 3¾x3, saucer 5½ in., thin transparent china, all over Japanese figure and landscape decoration, asstd. green & red gold decorated edges, 1 doz. in pkg. Per dozen, $1.25

L1550—Large size, cup 3¾x2, saucer 5⅛, transparent, rich allover blue print decorations. 1 doz. in pkg. Doz. $1.25

L2026—Cup 3¾x2, saucer 5⅜, hand painted roses, gold scroll work and tinted edges, gold traced handle. ½ doz. in pkg.......Doz. $1.65

L5011—3¾x2, saucer, 5½ extra quality transparent "Shapin" white china, floral and bird underglazed decorations in delicate green and pink. ½ doz. in pkg., Doz. Out

L44—Cup 3½x2¼, saucer 5½ in., thin transparent china, ovide shape, all over Japanese land and water outside decoration in colors, inlaid with gold. Tokio red edges. ½ doz. in pkg. Doz. Out

L5016—3¾x2, saucer 5½, thin white china, chrysanthemum and forget me not spray decoration, gold tracing, gold decorated cobalt blue edge. ½ doz. in pkg. Doz. $1.85

L5008—Cup 3⅞x2, saucer 5½ in., transparent china, Japanese figure and landscape gold traced decoration, wide irregular maroon & gold trimmed cobalt edges and handles. ½ doz. in pkg...Doz. $1.85

JAP CHINA AFTER DINNER C & S.

L1530 — Cup 3x1⅝, saucer 4½ in., Mino ware china, all over blue decoration. 1 doz. in pkg..............Doz. 42c

L1531—Diam. 3 in., saucer 4¼, low shape white ground, Japanese scenes and figures in asstd. colorings, Tokio red border and handle. 1 doz. in pkg.. ....Doz. 65c

L1535—Ovide, 2⅞x1⅝, saucer 4⅜, allover floral landscape and figure decorations, rich red band edges. 1 doz. in pkg......Doz. 85c

L2004—Cup 2½x2¼, saucer 4⅝, floral hand painted decorations, gold trimmings, asstd. blue, green and pink band edges, asstd. 6 decorations............Doz. 87c

INDIVIDUAL BUTTER PLATES.

L1690 L1691 L1692

L1690—Diam. 3¼ in. blue and white Sometsuke floral center with neat border. 1 doz. in box...........................Doz. 18c

L1691 — Diam. 3¼ in. Tokio red edges, figure and landscape allover decoration. 1 doz. in pkg...................... ......Doz. 24c

L1692—3½ in., deep dainty and gold sprays in wreath design, gold edge. Asstd. 3 styles. 1 doz. in pkg..........Doz. 36c

L1695 — Extra large diam. 4½ in., Tokio red and blue edges, figure and landscape decoration. 1 doz. in pkg. asstd......... ...Doz. 39c

JAPANESE CHINA BREAD AND BUTTER PLATES.

L1615—6¼ in., fancy allover blue decorations of birds, dragons, floral and scroll designs. 1 doz. in pkg..........Doz. Out

L1616—6 in. thin china, allover blue and white decoration. 1 doz. in pkg....Doz. Out

L1617 — 6 in., transparent china, fluted flange, asstd. 3 Japanese landscape and figure decorations, gold illuminated, red and green edges. 1 doz. in pkg., asstd. Doz. 85c

L5132—6 in., thin transparent china, allover hand painted flowers, landscapes and figures, gold trimmed cobalt blue band around edges. Doz. 95c

JAP CHINA TABLE PLATES.

L2239—7¼ in., fluted flange, asstd. floral decorations with gold tracings and sprays, gold pink or green edges. ½ doz. in pkg., asstd...Doz. $1.65

L2241—7¼ in., 2 styles, rose and chrysanthemum cluster, natural colors, gold lacework and tracings, deep cobalt blue edge, gold traced. ½ doz. in pkg...Doz. $1.75

L5142—7¼ in., fluted flange, cobalt beaded & gold traced edges. 2 floral decorations on tinted ground, gold lace effect & scrolls. ½ doz. in pkg., asstd. Doz. Out

DINNER PLATE ASST.

L41 — 8½ in., transparent china. fluted flanges, asstd. terra cotta, dark and light green banded scalloped edges, 2 fire Jap print decorations in several colors and asstd. subjects. ½ doz. in pkg..Dz. $2.25

JAPANESE FANCY BERRY, SALAD OR FRUIT BOWL ASST.

Cannot be duplicated today in the Japanese market.

L48—6 shapes and decorations, average 9½ in., extra fine Jap china, all over Japanese scenic decorations in many colors and gold, cobalt, Tokio red or green bands on scalloped edges. ¼ doz. in pkg. Per dozen. Out

JAPANESE CHINA BOWLS.

L1740—4¾x2¼ in., fireproof allover blue outside decoration, showing birds and flowers, fancy blue band round inner top and bottom. 1 doz. in pkg...... Doz. 36c

L5170 — 4⅝ in., deep fluted shape with foot, inside Japanese figures and landscape decoration in colors. Tokio red edge, 3 decorations. 1 doz. in pkg., asstd. Doz. 67c

L1746—6¼ in., fancy floral designs, allover blue outside decoration, fancy wide blue band around inside edge and bottom. 1 doz. in pkg. Doz. 89c

JAP CHINA TETE-A-TETE SETS.

L2300—Tea pot 6 in., sugar 4⅛, creamer 3¾ in., cups 3x1⅝, white china, allover Japanese figure and landscape decorations, Tokio red and gold edge, gold decorated handles. 1 set in box......... .....Set, Out

L5230—Tea pot 4¼, sugar 3¾, creamer 3 in., 2 cups 3x2¼, saucers 5 in., thin transparent china, floral and leaf decoration with gold filigree and scrolls, gold trimmed edges and handles. 1 set in box...............Set, 90c

JAPANESE CHINA CHOCOLATE SET.

L43 — 8 in. pot, six 2¼x2½ in. cups, and 5 in. saucers, transparent china, ribbed panel, scalloped edges, all over red, green, blue and gold 2-fire Japanese decorations, cups decorated inside. 1 set in box. Set. $1.35

JAPANESE CHINA FOOTED NUT BOWL.

L5047 — 5 in., fluted scallop shape, 2 styles, allover Japanese landscape and floral decoration, gold decorated red and green edges, outside sprays. 1 doz. in pkg. asstd.....Doz. $1.25

L64—6¼ in., white china, fancy scalloped shape, Jap figure and cherry blossom decoration, heavy gold ornamented Tokio red and gold edges, outside sprays. 3 in pkg....Each, 39c

Butler Bros. Catalog, 1909.

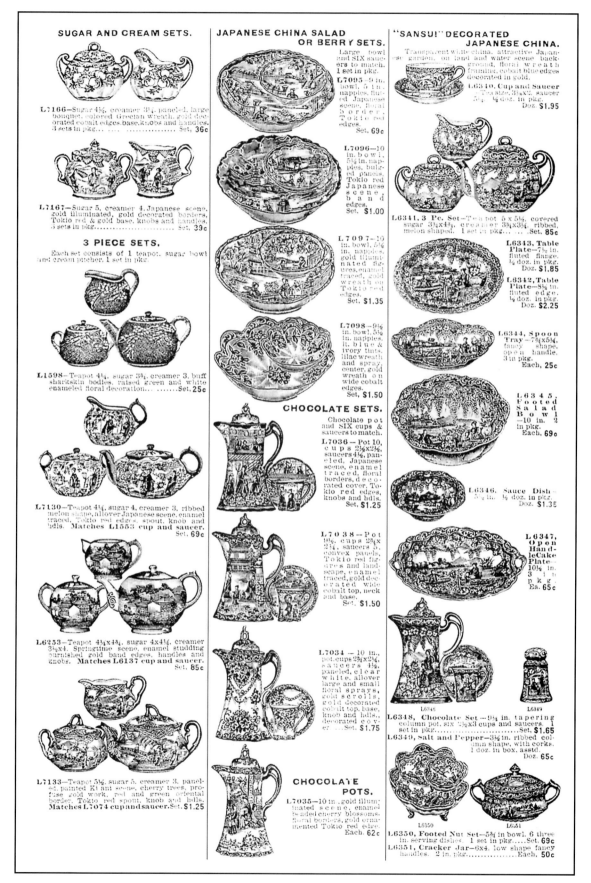

SUGAR AND CREAM SETS.

L7166—Sugar 4½, creamer 3½, panel-d, large bouquet, colored Grecian wreath, gold decorated cobalt edges, base, knobs and handles. 4 sets in pkg.... ...... Set, 36c

L7167—Sugar 5, creamer 4, Japanese scene, gold illuminated, gold decorated borders, Tokio red & gold base, knobs and handles. 5 sets in pkg....................... Set, 39c

3 PIECE SETS.

Each set consists of 1 teapot, sugar bowl and cream pitcher. 1 set in pkg.

L1598—Teapot 4½, sugar 3½, creamer 3, buff sharkskin bodies, raised green and white enameled floral decoration... ....Set, 25c

L7130—Teapot 4½, sugar 4, creamer 3, ribbed melon shape, allover Japanese scene, enamel traced, Tokio red edges, spout, knob and hdls. Matches L1553 cup and saucer. Set, 69c

L6253—Teapot 4½x4½, sugar 4x4½, creamer 3½x4, Springtime scene, enamel studding burnished gold band edges, handles and knobs. Matches L6137 cup and saucer. Set, 85c

L7133—Teapot 5½, sugar 5, creamer 3, panel-ed, painted Ki ani scene, cherry trees, profuse gold work, red and green oriental border, Tokio red spout, knob and hdls. Matches L7074 cup and saucer. Set, $1.25

JAPANESE CHINA SALAD OR BERRY SETS.

Large bowl and SIX saucers to match. 1 set in pkg.

L7095—9 in. bowl, 5 in. nappies, fluted Japanese scene, floral border. Tokio red edges. Set, 69c

L7096—10 in. bowl, 5½ in. nappies, bulged panels, Tokio red Japanese scene band edges. Set, $1.00

L7097—10 in. bowl, 5½ in. nappies, gold illuminated figures, enamel traced, gold wreath on Tokio red edges. Set, $1.35

L7098—9½ in. bowl, 5½ in. nappies, lt. blue & ivory tints, lilac wreath and spray, center, gold wreath on wide cobalt edges. Set, $1.50

CHOCOLATE SETS.

Chocolate pot and SIX cups & saucers to match.

L7036—Pot 10, cups 2½x2½, saucers 4½, paneled, Japanese scene, enamel traced, floral borders, decorated cover. Tokio red edges, knobs and hdls. Set, $1.25

L7038—Pot 9½, cups 2¾x 2½, saucers 5, convex panels, Tokio red figures and landscape, enamel traced, gold decorated wide cobalt top, neck and base. Set, $1.50

L7034—10 in. pot, cups 2¾x2½, saucers 4½, paneled, clear white, allover large and small floral sprays, gold scrolls, gold decorated cobalt top, base, knob and hdls., decorated cover. Set, $1.75

CHOCOLATE POTS.

L7035—10 in., gold illuminated scene, enamel beaded cherry blossoms, floral borders, gold ornamented Tokio red edge. Each. 62c

"SANSU!" DECORATED JAPANESE CHINA.

Transparent white china, attractive Japanese garden, on land and water scene background, floral wreath framing, cobalt blue edges decorated in gold.

L6340. Cup and Saucer—Tea size, 3½x2½, saucer 5½. ½ doz. in pkg. Doz. $1.95

L6341, 3 Pc. Set—Tea pot 5x5½, covered sugar 3½x4½, creamer 3½x3½, ribbed, melon shaped. 1 set in pkg... Set, 85c

L6343, Table Plate—7½ in. fluted flange. ½ doz. in pkg. Doz. $1.85

L6342, Table Plate—8½ in. fluted edge. ½ doz. in pkg. Doz. $2.25

L6344, Spoon Tray—7¾x5½, fancy shape, open handle. 3 in pkg. Each, 25c

L6345, Footed Salad Bowl—10 in. 2 in pkg. Each, 69c

L6346, Sauce Dish—5½ in. ½ doz. in pkg. Doz. $1.35

L6347, Open Handle Cake Plate—10½ in. 3 in pkg. Ea. 65c

L6348, Chocolate Set—9½ in. tapering column pot, six 3½x3 cups and saucers. 1 set in pkg. Set, $1.65

L6349, Salt and Pepper—3½ in. ribbed column shape, with corks. 1 doz. in box. asstd. Doz. 65c

L6350, Footed Nut Set—5¾ in. bowl, 6 three in. serving dishes. 1 set in pkg. Set, 69c

L6351, Cracker Jar—6x4, low shape, fancy handles. 2 in pkg. Each, 50c

Butler Bros. Catalog, 1911.

JAPANESE CHINA TABLE PLATES

L1625—7¼ in clear white china, blue and white peonies. Matches L1549 cup and saucer. 1 doz. pkg.....Doz. 96c

L7622—7¼ in. Geisha and floral decoration, fluted flange, Tokio red edge. Matches L7567 cup and saucer, and L7772 three pc. set......Doz. 96c

L7614—7¼ in. gold illuminated Japanese figure and garden, gold ornamented Tokio red edge. Matches L7556 cup and saucer. Doz. $1.80

L7147—8¼ in. fluted flange, allover gold illuminated Japanese scene, enamel studded cherry blossoms. Tokio red and gold edge. ½ doz. pkg. Doz. $2.15

INDIVIDUAL BUTTER PLATES.
1 doz. pkg.

L7027 L7611 L7029

L7027—3¼ in., 2 blue and white Sometsuke decorations. Asstd. Doz. 15c

L7611 — 3¼ in., allover Japanese landscape and figures, red edge. Dz. Out

L7029 — 3¼ in., 3 floral decorations, gold sprays, red, green and pink edges. Asstd...Doz. 25c

L7612—4¼ in., floral and figured decoration, bright red edge.........Doz. 35c

1L7612

EGG CUPS—1 doz. pkg.

L5036—1¾x2⅛, allover Japanese scene, Tokio red edge..............Doz. 33c

1L5037—2¾ x 3¼, allover Japanese scene, Tokio red and gold edges..Doz. 78c

L5036 L5037

JAP CHINA INDIVIDUAL NUT BOWL.

L7651—3x1¼, ribbed figured and landscape design, Tokio red border and feet. 1 doz. pkg. Doz. 36c

FOOTED NUT BOWLS.

L7658 L7657

L7658—4½ in. clear white, 2 designs, floral borders and centers, gold sprays and decorated edges, cobalt edges and feet. 1 doz. pkg.........Doz. 89c

L7657 — 5¾ in. allover Jap figures and flower garden, Tokio red edge and feet. 1 doz. pkg. Doz. $1.25

L7668—7 in. bulge panels, Japanese tea garden, floral border. Tokio red edge and feet. ½ doz. pkg. Doz. $2.00

L7668

L7663 — 7½ in. paneled, lt. blue tint, 3 enamel traced pink and rose bouquets and outlined foliage, gold lattice, enamel beaded green band outline, gold overlaid, cobalt blue edge and feet. Each, 36c

JAPANESE CHINA FANCY BONBON OR OLIVE DISHES.

L5060 — 5½ in. ribbed, clear white china, 3 hand painted floral decorations, gold ornamented, cobalt edges. 1 doz. pkg........Doz. 89c

1L7677—8 in. panels, gold illuminated Japanese figure and landscape, green band and floral border, gold ornamented, Tokio red edge and feet. ½ doz. in pkg. Doz. $2.25

L7124 — 7½ in. transparent white china ornamental gold framed berry medallions, pansies, green foliage, in cobalt and gold edge inside and out. ¼ pkg. Each, 36c

L7775 — Tea pot 7¼, sugar 6, creamer 5¼ in., allover Japanese figure and floral landscape decoration, Tokio red edges, handles and spout.................... ....Set, Out

L7771—Tea pot 8, sugar 6¼, creamer 5¼, tinted land and marine scene, maroon band border with colored inlays, black base bands, gold line edges, knob and handle....Set, 95c

L6802—As L7771, with 6 cups and saucers to match....................Complete, $2.00

L7769 — Tea pot 7¾, sugar 6, creamer 5, marine, island and mountain scene pastel tints, enameled cherry blossoms, lt. green conventional borders and base, gold edges, decorated hdls., spout and knobs..........Set, $1.25

L6803—As L7769, with 6 cups and saucers to match ....Complete, $2.25

L7770 — Tea pot 8, sugar 6, creamer 5¼, swell panel, dk. green, tan and ivory blending, hand painted enamel traced pink, yellow and red rose bouquets, gold veined and outlined foliage, beaded gold mounted cobalt borders, and decorated base, hdls., knob and spout...........................Set, $1.75

L6806 — As L7770, with 6 cup and saucers to match............ ....Complete, $3.75

JAPANESE CHINA CHOCOLATE SETS.

Chocolate pot and 6 cups and saucers to match.

L7782—Pot 10 cups, 2⅛x3, saucers 5 in., paneled, allover Japanese figure and floral design in colors, decorated top, Tokio red knobs, edges and handle. Set, $1.25

L7780—Pot 10, cups 2⅛x3, saucers 5 in., paneled, light blue and ivory tints, hand painted lilacs, enameled centers, gold ornamented cobalt blue edges and handles. Set, $1.75

L7786—Pot 10, cups 2⅛x3, saucers 5 in. Japanese tea garden and Geisha design, enameled floral border, gold over blue cobalt top, edges and handles. Set, $1.50

L7781 — Pot 10, cups 2⅛x3 saucers 5 in. paneled, swell base, lt. green and white tinted, conventional rose clusters, back outlined gold bands, gold ornamented edges and handles. Set, $1.85

JAPANESE CHINA MUSTARD POT.

1 doz. pkg. With spoons.

L7706 L7705

L7706—3¼ in. Japanese figure decoration. Tokio red edges, knob and handle........... ....Doz. 89c

L7705—4 in., clear white china, enamel traced floral decoration, gold sprays, gold lined handles. ....Doz. 95c

Butler Bros. Catalog, 1912.

LARKIN PREMIUMS GIVEN WITH PURCHASES OF LARKIN PRODUCTS DESCRIBED ON PAGES 9 TO 43   147

Imported Hand-Painted China

Chocolate Set

No. K219 GIVEN with a $3.80 purchase of Products or for $3.80 in Coupons.

Consists of 9½-in. Chocolate Pot and six Cups and Saucers. Decorated with pink flowers, green leaves and white embossed work on chocolate-color background. Gilt edges and handles. Shipping weight 8 lbs.

Cake Set

No. 7915 GIVEN with a $3 purchase of Products or for $3 in Coupons.

A handsome Cake or Bread-and-Butter Set that matches Chocolate Set K219.

Set consists of one 10-in. Cake-Plate and six 6-in. individual Plates. Decoration is pink flowers, green leaves and white embossed work on chocolate-color background. Edges are gilt. Shipping weight 8 lbs.

Nut Set

No. 418 GIVEN with a $3.60 purchase of Products or for $3.60 in Coupons.

Set consists of one 6-in. Bowl and six 2⅝-in. individual Bowls. Decoration is white flowers and green leaves outlined in gold. Edges traced in gold. Shipping weight 5 lbs.

Cups and Saucers Set

No. 714 GIVEN with a $2.80 purchase of Products or for $2.80 in Coupons.

Six Teacups and six Saucers. Decoration consists of gold roses and panels of scroll-work, with pink roses and green leaves. Shipping weight 6 lbs.

Mayonnaise Set

No. 909 GIVEN with a $1.80 purchase of Products or for $1.80 in Coupons.

Set consists of a Ladle, a 5-in. Bowl and a 6¼-in. Plate. Has a border design of light-blue and pink flowers on a moire band in gold ribbon-effect. Shipping weight 2 lbs.

Jam Jar Set

No. 49010 GIVEN with a $2 purchase of Products or for $2 in Coupons.

Set consists of Jar, 3¾ in. high, Plate 6¾ in. in diameter, and Ladle. Decorated with pink, white and red roses, blended with shaded leaves. Edges are outlined in gold. Shipping weight 3 lbs.

Bon Bon Dish

No. K1110 GIVEN with a $2 purchase of Products or for $2 in Coupons.

Diameter, 7 in. Inside decoration consists of a landscape with lilies in natural colors in the foreground. Has fancy gold border outside. Burnished gold edges and handles. Shipping weight 3 lbs.

Sugar and Cream Set

No. K109 GIVEN with a $1.80 purchase of Products or for $1.80 in Coupons.

Decoration consists of combination border-and-spray design of berries and leaves in delicate tints of blue, green and red, traced in gold. Gold handles and edges. Height, 3 in. Diameter of Sugar-Bowl, 4 in.; Cream-Pitcher, 3½ in. Shipping weight 2 lbs.

Condiment Set

No. 709 GIVEN with a $1.80 purchase of Products or for $1.80 in Coupons.

Set consists of Tray, 7x5 in., Mustard-Jar with Spoon, Tooth-Pick-Holder and Salt- and Pepper-Shakers. Decoration is a conventional design in burnished gold. Shipping weight 2 lbs.

Tea-Plate Set

No. 2012 GIVEN with a $2.40 purchase of Products or for $2.40 in Coupons.

Set consists of six Plates, 7½ in. in diameter. Prettily decorated with gold roses and panels of scroll-work, with pink roses and green leaves. Matches Cups and Saucers Set 714. Shipping weight 5 lbs.

Jelly Set

No. 56010 GIVEN with a $2 purchase of Products or for $2 in Coupons.

Set consists of one handled Plate, 7¼ in. in diameter, and six individual Dishes. Conventional border design of green leaves and flowers, richly illuminated in raised gold. Edges outlined in gold. Matches Celery Set 1513. Makes an excellent butter or nut set. Shpg. wt. 2 lbs.

Celery Set

No. 1513 GIVEN with a $2.60 purchase of Products or for $2.60 in Coupons.

Set consists of one Celery Tray, 12¾ x 6¼ in., and six individual Salt-Trays. Decorated in a conventional border design of green leaves and flowers, richly illuminated in raised gold. Edges outlined with gold. Shipping weight 3 lbs.

Puff-Box and Hair-Receiver Set

No. 5405 GIVEN with a $1 purchase of Products or for $1 in Coupons.

Conventional border-design of pink flowers and green leaves, richly illuminated with gold. Diameter, 3½ in. Shipping weight 2 lbs.

Dresser Set

No. 717A GIVEN with a $3.50 purchase of Products or for $3.50 in Coupons.

Set consists of Brush-and-Comb-Tray, 7⅜ x 10⅜ in.; Pin-Tray; Puff-Box; Hair-Receiver; Hat-Pin-Holder. Decoration is pink roses and green leaves with embossed work in gold. Shipping weight 6 lbs.

Manicure Set

No. K609 GIVEN with a $1.80 purchase of Products or for $1.80 in Coupons.

Set consists of 7¼-in. Tray, oblong Powder-Box and three different size jars that can be used for cold cream, powdered pumice, cuticle-ice, etc. Decoration is pink roses and green leaves with embossed work in gold. Matches Dresser Set 717A. Shipping weight 2 lbs.

All Premiums May be EARNED BY SENDING CLUB ORDERS   Read How on Pages 4 and 5

Larkin Catalog, 1916

IMPORTED CHINA SUGAR AND CREAM SETS

E5456—3 styles, large shapes, sugar aver. 3¾ in., creamer 3, attractive floral border decors., gold edges striped handles and knobs. Asstd. ½ doz. sets in pkg.
Doz. sets, **$7.30**

7 PC. SALAD OR BERRY SET
Attractive pattern in good color combinations.

L6364—Bowl 10, SIX fruits 5½, enamel traced pink tinted crimped edge and floral clusters, connecting gold traced buff bands, enamel beaded inner band, center spray. 1 set in pkg.
SET (7 pcs.), $1.40

3 PC. IMPORTED CHINA DRESSER SET
The uncommon beauty of these dainty hand painted dresser sets appeals to women at once. Mark them in odd figures.

L6430—3 pcs., tray 7¾ x3¼, hair receiver and puff jar 3¾ x2½, dome covers, embossed, enamel traced pink floral sprays, gold tendrils and edges. 2 sets in pkg. SET (3 pcs.), **45c**

4 PC. IMPORTED CHINA SMOKERS' SET
Use some of these prominently in your Holiday display.

L6535—4 pcs., tray 7⅛, cigar holder 2⅞, match holder 1⅝, ash tray 2½. white enamel traced brown band, allover Japanese scenic design. 1 set in box. SET (4 pcs.), **56c**

L7172—Bowl 9¾ in., 6 fruits 5½ in., grouped pink floral design, alternate blue gold traced medallion & connecting green vine, gold edges. 1 set in pkg...SET (7 pcs.), $1.35

E5458—Sugar 3½ in., creamer 3 in., tinted ground with large rose and foliage bouquet, trailing buds, gold dec. handles and knobs. ¼ doz. sets in pkg.
Doz. sets, **$8.75**

E1131—2 styles, sugar aver. 3½ in., creamer 3 in., new shape copied from the French, conventional floral designs, green and pink band edges, gold traced and half matt handles, gold enameled flowers. Asstd. 2 sets in pkg...(Total $3.00) Set. **$1.50**

E6182—Tea pot 5 in., cov. sugar 4 in., creamer 3 in., 6 cups 3¾ x2 in., saucer 5¼ in., violet cluster spray on cream background, light blue band border, gold line handles and knobs. 1 set in pkg.
SET (9 pcs.), **$4.25**

IMPORTED CHINA INDIVIDUAL FOOTED SALT DIP
Can be used for nuts

E7460—2⅜ in., hexagon footed shape, gold edges and illuminated sides. 2 doz. in pkg...............Doz. **72c**
(Total $1.44)

IMPORTED CHINA CONDIMENT SETS

E6395—6 pcs., salt and pepper 2⅞, toothpick holder 2, mustard pot 3, floral festooning, enamel beaded band, gold scrolls, edges and dec. knob. ½ doz. sets in box.
Doz. sets, **$4.90**

E5468—3 styles, covd. sugar, aver. 3¼ in., creamer aver. 3 in., white china, asstd. floral sprays and clusters with gold dec., cream panel effects and fancy gold tracings, gold handles, edges, base lines and knobs. Asstd. ¼ doz. sets in pkg. Doz. sets, **$14.00**

E4925—Creamer 2¾ in., sugar 3¾, delicate pink & white roses, green foliage, on gold outlined gray band, allover ivory tint, wide coin gold ornamented edges, knobs and handles. 2 sets in pkg.........Set. **$2.25**
(Total $4.50)

IMPORTED CHINA TABLEWARE SPECIALTIES

E4931

E4933

Good quality, light wt. highly glazed translucent body, hand painted effect, pink shaded roses, green foliage border.
E4932—Cup 3x2⅜, saucer 5¾. 1 doz. in pkg.
Doz. **$4.25**
E4931—Sauce dish, 5¼ in. 1 doz. in pkg.
Doz. **$1.75**
E4933—Table plate, 7¾ in. 1 doz. in pkg.
Doz. **$3.50**

IMPORTED CHINA CREAM PITCHERS

E5408—2 styles, 3 in., floral and gold decor. and sprays, gold edges. Asstd. 1 doz. in pkg............Doz. **$1.50**

E5410—2 styles, 3¾ in., floral and violet medallion decoration and brown band, gold edges and handle. Asstd. ½ doz. in pkg......Doz. **$3.50**

E5409 — Ht. 3¾ in., good grade china body, panel sides, tankard shape, blue pastel pale tinted bands. Hand painted pink rose spray with gold line edge and handle. 1 doz. in pkg...Doz. **$3.75**

E7929 — 2 styles, 4⅜ in., panel sides, blue pastel pale tinted bands, pink rose and violet decor. in natural colors, gold edges, inner verge line and around base. Asstd. ½ doz. in pkg...Doz. **$4.00**

IMPORTED CHINA SYRUP PITCHER

E5648—Ht. 3¾ in., new shape, delicate pink roses and wildflowers with lavender stems, pale blue pastel band border, gold traced handles & knobs. ½ doz. in pkg..Doz. **$13.50**

E5452—Sugar 3¾ in., creamer 3½ in., new shape, allover Japanese figure and landscape decors., Tokio red edges and handles. ½ doz. sets in pkg........Doz. sets, **$6.90**

Butler Bros. Catalog, 1919 – 1920.

L5211—Kochi Asst., 36 shapes, 2 decors., comprises plates, bonbon and pickle dishes, nut bowls, hair receivers and puff boxes, hatpin holders, sugar and cream sets, mayonnaise sets, rose jars, toothbrush holders, sugar shakers, cream and syrup pitchers, candlestick holders, pin and ash trays, fancy shapes, rose medallion with gold outlined old ivory scrolls, gold dec. lt. blue border; gold traced orient. medallion, gold traced lt. blue band, gold edges & dec. hdls. Asstd. 6 doz. in case, 70 lbs. **Doz. $2.25**
(Total for asst. $13.50)

L5210—"Variety" Asst., 19 styles, comprises chocolate, berry and tea sets, cups and saucers (count as 1 pc.), plates, mustard pot, nut bowls and dishes, puff box and hair receivers, sugar shakers, salts and peppers and hatpin holders. White china enameled traced hand painted floral and Japanese landscape decorations. Retail range 10c to $1.00. **Doz. $1.08**
12 doz. in case, 120 lbs.   (Total for asst. $12.96)

AWATA VASE ASSORTMENTS

L5222—9 styles, ht. 10 in., tinted and mottled bodies, floral and landscape decors. gold frames, borders, ornaments and hdls. 3 doz. in case, 174 lbs. ....**Doz. $5.00**

CHINA TOOTHPICK HOLDERS

L6470—2¼ in., conventional decoration, maroon edge. 1 doz. in box ..... Doz. 3c

L6471—2¼ in., 2 styles and shapes, gold decorated traced conventional design, gold edge. Asstd. 1 doz. in pkg. Doz. 5c

CHINA SPOON TRAY, PICKLE OR RELISH DISH ASSTS.

L6252—2 styles, 7¾ in., open hdls., gold traced tan border and floral inlays, gold traced roses on combination tints, beaded gold edge. Asstd. ½ doz. in pkg. Doz. $4.00

L1037—3 styles, aver. 7¾x4¼, white china, gold decor. floral borders with tinted outer band. gold edges. Asstd. ¼ doz. in pkg. Doz. $4.20

CHINA OLIVE, BONBON OR NUT DISH ASSTS.

L1031 — 3 styles, aver. 5½x4¼, white china, gold ornamented floral borders. Asstd. ½ doz. in pkg. ....Doz. $2.25

L744—12 styles, aver. 5x7, white china, floral bouquets, landscape and conventional border designs. profuse gold ornamentation. Asstd. 1 doz. in pkg. ....Doz. $6.00

CHINA BISCUIT OR CRACKER JARS

L7490—4¼x6¼. pink rose and foliage sprays connecting gold scroll band, gold decor. edges, hdls. and knobs. ¼ doz. in pkg. ....Doz. $9.00

L6528—6¼x6 in., hand painted gold outlined blossom buds and leaves on long stems, shaded in vari-color, brown figured, ivory border, gold ornaments, gold lined handles. 1 in pkg. ....Each, 95c

Butler Bros. Catalog, 1917 – 1918.

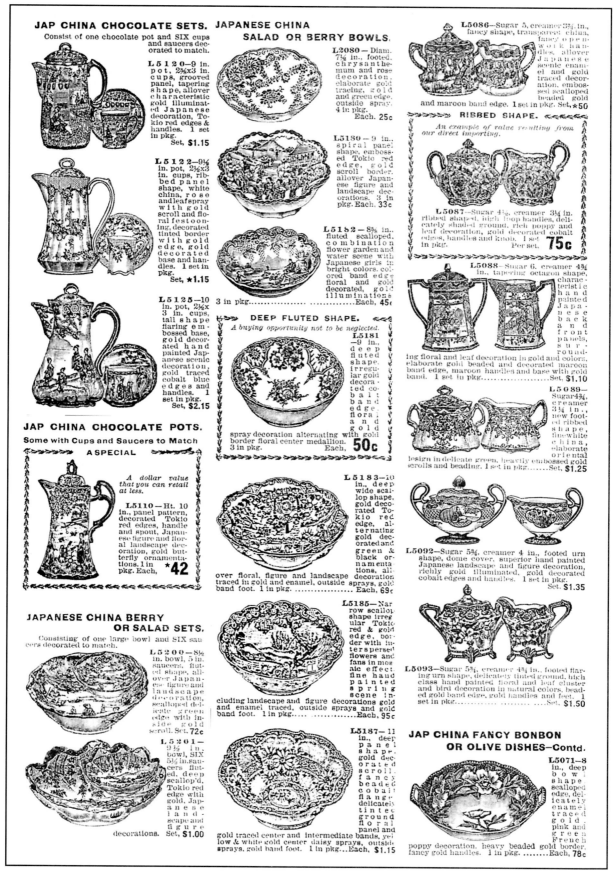

JAP CHINA CHOCOLATE SETS.

Consist of one chocolate pot and SIX cups and saucers decorated to match.

L5120—9 in. pot, 2⅜x3 in. cups, grooved panel, tapering shape, allover characteristic gold illuminated Japanese decoration, Tokio red edges & handles. 1 set in pkg. Set, $1.15

L5122—9½ in. pot, 2½x3 in. cups, ribbed panel shape, white china, rose and leaf spray with gold scroll and floral festooning, decorated tinted border with gold edge, decorated base and handles. 1 set in pkg. Set, ★1.15

L5125—10 in. pot, 2½x3 in. cups, tall shape flaring embossed base, gold decorated hand painted Japanese scenic decoration, gold traced cobalt blue edges and handles. 1 set in pkg. Set, $2.15

JAP CHINA CHOCOLATE POTS.

Some with Cups and Saucers to Match

A SPECIAL

A dollar value that you can retail at less.

L5110—Ht. 10 in., panel pattern, decorated Tokio red edges, handle and spout, Japanese figure and floral landscape decoration, gold butterfly ornamentations. 1 in pkg. Each, ★42

JAPANESE CHINA BERRY OR SALAD SETS.

Consisting of one large bowl and SIX saucers decorated to match.

L5200—8½ in. bowl, 5 in. saucers, fluted shape, allover Japanese figure and landscape decoration, scalloped delicate green edge with inside gold scroll. Set. 72c

L5201—9¾ in. bowl, SIX 5½ in. saucers fluted, deep scallop'd, Tokio red edge with gold, Japanese landscape and figure decorations. Set, $1.00

JAPANESE CHINA SALAD OR BERRY BOWLS.

L2080—Diam. 7½ in., footed, chrysanthemum and rose decoration, elaborate gold tracing, gold and green edge, outside spray. 4 in pkg. Each. 25c

L5180—9 in., spiral panel shape, embossed Tokio red edge, gold scroll border, allover Japanese figure and landscape decorations. 3 in pkg. Each, 33c

L5182—8⅝ in., fluted scalloped, combination flower garden and water scene with Japanese girls in bright colors, colored band edge, floral and gold decorated, gold illuminations. Each, 45c

DEEP FLUTED SHAPE.
A buying opportunity not to be neglected.

L5181—9 in., deep fluted shape, irregular gold decorated cobalt band edge, floral and gold spray decoration alternating with gold border floral center medallion. 3 in pkg. Each, 50c

L5183—10 in., deep wide scallop shape, gold decorated Tokio red edge, alternating gold decorated and green & black ornamentations, allover floral, figure and landscape decoration traced in gold and enamel, outside sprays, gold band foot. 1 in pkg. Each, 69c

L5185—Narrow scallop shape irregular Tokio red & gold edge, border with interspersed flowers and fans in mosaic effect, fine hand painted spring scene including landscape and figure decorations gold and enamel traced, outside sprays and gold band foot. 1 in pkg. Each, 95c

L5187—11 in., deep panel shape, gold decorated scroll, fancy beaded cobalt flange, delicately tinted ground floral panel and gold traced center and intermediate bands, yellow & white gold center daisy sprays, outside sprays, gold band foot. 1 in pkg. Each, $1.15

L5086—Sugar 5, creamer 3¾ in., fancy shape, transparent china, fancy openwork handles, allover Japanese scenic enamel and gold traced decoration, embossed scalloped beaded gold and maroon band edge. 1 set in pkg. Set, ★50

RIBBED SHAPE.
An example of value resulting from our direct importing.

L5087—Sugar 4½, creamer 3¾ in. ribbed shape, high loop handles, delicately shaded ground, rich poppy and leaf decoration, gold decorated cobalt edges, handles and knob. 1 set in pkg. Per set. 75c

L5088—Sugar 6, creamer 4¾ in., tapering octagon shape, characteristic hand painted Japanese back and front panels, surrounding floral and leaf decoration in gold and colors, elaborate gold beaded and decorated maroon band edge, maroon handles and base with gold band. 1 set in pkg. Set, $1.10

L5089—Sugar 4½, creamer 3¼ in., new footed ribbed shape, fine white china, elaborate oriental design in delicate green, heavily embossed gold scrolls and beading. 1 set in pkg. Set, $1.25

L5092—Sugar 5¾, creamer 4 in., footed urn shape, dome cover, superior hand painted Japanese landscape and figure decoration, richly gold illuminated, gold decorated cobalt edges and handles. 1 set in pkg. Set. $1.35

L5093—Sugar 5¾, creamer 4½ in., footed flaring urn shape, delicately tinted ground, high class hand painted floral and leaf cluster and bird decoration in natural colors, beaded gold band edge, gold handles and feet. 1 set in pkg. Set, $1.50

JAP CHINA FANCY BONBON OR OLIVE DISHES—Contd.

L5071—8 in., deep bowl shape scalloped edge, delicately enamel traced gold, pink and green French poppy decoration, heavy beaded gold border, fancy gold handles. 1 in pkg. Each, 78c

Remember those little green stamps? Years ago, we got them when we made a purchase at the local gas station or grocery market. They were pasted in the booklets provided by S&H and when the required amount had been saved they could be redeemed at the local Sperry & Hutchinson redemption center for an array of goodies. What fun! Something for free!

So what does this have to do with Nippon era (1891 – 1921) porcelain? Recently when I was on one of my shopping expeditions, I found a large, heavily enameled, jeweled vase that had a paper sticker affixed to the bottom. A large 18" vase is always exciting to locate, but one bearing a sticker with "This premium given in exchange for three books filled with the Sperry and Hutchinson green trading stamps" printed on it was really a find. The vase has a blue maple leaf backstamp that indicates manufacture between 1891 – 1911 by the Morimuras/Noritake Co. in Nagoya, Japan. It's about 100 years old, and the sticker never got washed off during this entire time period!

S&H began issuing trading stamps (small pieces of gummed paper) in 1896. The first redemption center opened in 1897 so that dates this particular vase between 1897 and 1911. S&H sold its stamps to retailers for use as customer incentives. The retailers gave the stamps to consumers, typically at a rate of one for each ten cents worth of purchases as a bonus for their patronage. Consumers would then paste the stamps in books of 1,200 and exchange the books for "gifts" at S&H redemption centers.

Although S&H stamps are no longer being given out nationwide as in the past, the Sperry and Hutchinson Co. is still in business. And yes, people still are pasting green stamps in books. But the company has also gone high tech. You can now use a small card about the size of a credit card when you make your purchase. It's swiped on a machine and the number of the stamps you earned is automatically tallied and recorded for future redemption. No more Saturday afternoons spent pasting stamps in those little books!

The Sperry and Hutchinson Company presently has an office in New York City, and in their lobby one can view an old Rolodex that was once used at a redemption center during the early years. They have no old catalogs from the Nippon era in their files, but the cards used in the Rolodex are large, approximately 7½" x 13½" in size, and featured all types of items from paintings to pickle casters, and yes, there were Japanese items. Although the Rolodex is locked in a plastic case, one of the employees was kind enough to go through the cards and photocopy those featuring Nippon items.

18" vase that has S&H sticker on bottom (shown below).

The first cards of the Rolodex have printed: "Just look at the premiums on the next page – don't you wish you had one? It's easy! They cost you nothing." "Collect S&H Green Stamps. Delay is waste. Begin earning a valuable premium today by collecting 'S&H' Green Stamps." Only two cards had Nippon era items featured, but what a treat it was to see the premiums given years ago.

It's been known that Nippon items were given as premiums for both the Larkin and Jewel Tea Company, but now S&H can be added to this list.

From the Sperry and Hutchinson Company archives is a news article featured in *The Daily Chronicle* in 1897. It shows a photo of the first S&H Redemption Center that was opened in February of that year. The article goes on to say:

"Sensational new notion of Sperry Hutchinson is really catching on! They call them green stamps, and they're going through the roof.

"It's a brand new idea in marketing and it's catching on like crazy. Some industry bigs predict it could transform the whole business if its success rate keeps up this pace.

"S&H Green Stamps is what the new company calls its concept. It is so simple and yet so effective that the main question being asked is why didn't anybody think of it before?

"Picture this. You're about to leave the store after buying your usual weekly groceries and the clerk hands you some little green stamps. The more groceries you buy, the more stamps you get. When you get home, you paste them into a booklet provided by the S&H people.

"When you have enough stamps, you take your books to a special shop and redeem them for a gift. A real nice gift, too, if the S&H catalogue is anything to go by.

"Sperry and Hutchinson, the clever new corporation that thought up the notion told me that the catalogue will be regularly updated with some of the finest brand names in the country gracing its pages.

"How does it work? Amazingly simple. The benefits to the retailer are just as great as those to the average Joe like you and me. The terrific giveaways so attract clientele that market owners are posting record sales. And all because of the little stamps."

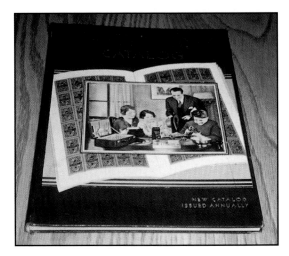

S&H Green Stamp Merchants Redemption Catalog from early 1920s.

Left:
Old Rolodex in lobby of S&H Company in New York City.

Right:
Close-up of Rolodex.

62

Nippon Patterns, Designs, Décors, and Scenes
by Mark Griffin

This chapter is an effort to help Nippon collectors and dealers identify the scenes, décors, patterns, and designs found on their items. Photos accompany each description.

1. **Gold scroll portraits:** One of the most commonly found portrait décors, it is typified by a portrait medallion surrounded by gold scrollwork on a cream background. These pieces are generally marked with blue #52 but are occasionally found unmarked. This decoration is most commonly found on vases, plates, and occasionally on tea set pieces.

2. **Red Cardinal:** One of the scarcer portrait décors features a Cardinal dressed in red. The portrait can be found facing in three different directions, with a combination of both white and brown clay moriage decorating the piece. Carrying the blue 52 mark, the décor is most commonly found on tankards, mugs, whiskey jugs, humidors, and plaques.

3. **Aqua jeweled Queen Louise:** The crown jewel of portrait pieces, this décor features a medallion of Queen Louise over a glossy aqua glaze accented with heavy gold and enameled jewelling. Items carry the blue #52 mark and the décor is only found on vases and urns.

4. **Enameled Indians:** Features famous American Indian Chiefs and is popular with both Indian décor collectors and collectors of smoking items. All pieces carry medallions featuring Indian Chiefs with enamel moriage trim work. Carrying the blue #47 mark, this décor is only seen on smoking items such as humidors, ashtrays, and cigarette boxes.

5. **Enameled grape portraits:** These portraits feature various male characters standing behind a stone wall. The pieces are accented by enameled grape vines and grapes. Carrying the green #47 mark, items are generally jugs and steins.

6. **Moriage portrait monks:** This décor features portrait monks surrounded by heavy brown moriage accented with white. Carrying the blue #52 mark, this décor is most commonly found on mugs, jugs, and vases on rare occasion.

1.

2.

3.

4.

5.

6.

7. **Floribunda tapestry:** One of the more commonly seen tapestry décors, it features large, plush pink and yellow roses. Generally marked with the blue #52 mark, pieces are occasionally found unmarked and this decoration is known to exist on vases, ewers, and chargers.

8. **Swan tapestry:** One of the less common scenes in the tapestry family, this décor features two swans on a pond, painted in pale yellow and green tones. Carrying the blue #52 backstamp, this décor is found on vases, ewers, and humidors.

9. **Grape tapestry:** Featuring grapes on the vine, this tapestry décor is painted in soft pastel tones of green and purple with the collars of the pieces done in heavy gold in relief. Bearing the blue #52 mark, this decoration is only known to exist on ewers and vases.

10. **Deco pendant tapestry:** Featuring pastel deco pendants with jewels, this décor is only known to exist on vases and carries the blue #52 mark. **Hunt scene tapestry:** This décor features an English hunt scene with dogs. Only known to exist on ewers and vases, these pieces carry the blue #52 mark. **Wisteria tapestry:** Featuring wisteria painted in soft lavender and green tones, this décor bears the blue #52 mark and is only seen on vases.

11. **Peach tapestry:** Painted with lush ripening peaches surrounded by leaves, this tapestry décor is only found on vases and covered urns and carries the blue #52 mark.

12. **Halloween tapestry:** One of the most rare of the tapestry décors, this scene is painted in bright pastel tones depicting a stylized village. This decoration is known to exist on humidors, ewers, and vases and carries the blue #52 mark.

7.

8.

9.

10.

11.

12.

13. **Pink lily tapestry:** Pink lily tapestry depicts newly blooming lilies and is only known to exist on vases. Pieces carry the blue #52 mark.

14. **Day on the pond tapestry:** Generally regarded as one of the best tapestry patterns, a Day on the Pond features a man and women preparing for a day of boating and done in soft pastel tones of blues, greens, and yellows. All pieces feature heavy gold work in relief around the tops and bottoms. These pieces carry the blue #52 mark and this scene is found on vases, humidors, and ewers.

15. **Castle on the lake tapestry:** This décor, done in coarse tapestry, is reminiscent of an old English castle beside a lake. Only known to exist on vases and ewers, pieces carry the blue #52 mark.

16. **Blue Gallé tapestry:** Unlike the traditional orange Galle décor, this variation is painted in soft pastel shades of blue and lavender. Pieces exhibit extensive collar enameling and lavender trees done in enamel moriage. This decoration has only been found on vases. These pieces carry the blue #52 mark.

17. **Enchanted forest:** This scene depicts a stylized scene of a house and stream. Known to exist on a large number of vases, humidors, and jugs. These pieces carry the green #47 mark.

18. **Green swan scene:** This soft pastel décor scene of two swans on a lake has a light green background. The scene also features gold leaves in overlay. Executed on a large number of molds including vases, plaques, chocolate sets, and urns this décor carries the blue #52 mark.

13.

14.

15.

19. Heidi herding ducks: A stylized Dutch scene of a girl herding ducks, this scene is found on vases, dresser sets, plaques, and humidors, and carries the blue #47 or green #47 mark.

16.

17.

18.

19.

20. **Jeweled cobalt portraits:** This scene depicts various portrait medallions of Victorian women over cobalt, heavily adorned with gold and jewelling. Known to exist on plaques and various molds of vases. These pieces carry the blue #52 mark.

21. **Jeweled moriage portraits:** This décor features medallions of Victorian women over a two-toned field of tan and brown on a green background. Decorated with white clay moriage and multicolored jewelling, pieces carry the blue #52 mark. This decoration is known to exist on vases and urns.

22. **White enameled portraits:** This décor consists of medallions of various scenes including Victorian women, monks, and hunt scenes over a field of white. Known to exist only on jugs and humidors, all pieces are trimmed with fine enamel beading and carry the blue #52 mark.

23. **Golden ivy portrait:** This décor consists of medallions of Victorian women over a field of white with gold and pink ivy overlay. Known to exist on various vase molds and ewers, pieces are generally unmarked.

24. **Pastel poppy coralene:** Done in soft pastels of pink, green, and lavender, this décor can be found with and without cobalt trim. Only known to exist on various molds of vases and carries patent mark #245.

25. **Golden mum coralene:** With a background fading from soft golden to pastel blue, these pieces are decorated with bi-colored golden mums. Known to exist on various vase molds and cracker jars. These items carry the patent marks #242 or #245.

20.

21.

22.

23.

24.

25.

26. Bleeding heart coralene: With a background of pale yellow fading to pale green, pieces are decorated with soft pink and purple bleeding hearts and vines. Known only to exist on vases and carries patent marks #242 or #245.

27. Cypress village coralene: Featuring a village by a lake decorated with coralene beading. Cypress village is one of the more coveted coralene décors. This decoration is only known to exist on vases and carries patent mark #242.

28. Lavender hollyhocks coralene: On a lavender background, pieces feature lavender and white hollyhocks and pale green leaves. This decoration is only known to exist on vases and carries patent mark #242.

29. Cobalt lilies coralene: Stunning multicolored lilies over a mottled green background with cobalt trim makes these desirable pieces for collectors. Known to exist on urns, ewers, and vases. These pieces carry patent mark #242.

30. Spring hollyhocks coralene: Generally done on larger molds, pieces feature pink and white hollyhocks on a field of mottled green. This décor has been found on tankards, urns, and larger vases. They carry patent mark #245.

31. Sweet pea coralene: Pieces feature a bank of sweet peas on a field of golden browns, and this decoration has only been found on vases carrying patent #245.

26.

27.

28.

32. Cobalt jeweled country road: One of the more stunning cobalt décors, pieces feature a rust tone scene of a country road over a field of cobalt and gold. Known to exist on urns, vases, chocolate and tea sets, and plaques. They carry blue mark #52.

29.

30.

31.

32.

33. Cobalt orchid: Large plushy pink orchids in a medallion are the hallmark of this cobalt and gold overlay décor. Known to exist on various molds of vases, these pieces carry the blue #52 mark.

34. Cobalt cherry tree: Featuring cobalt and silver overlay trim, these pieces are painted with a cherry tree beside a lake. Known to exist on various molds of vases, humidors, and tea sets, pieces carry the RC mark.

35. Cobalt swan: Another sought after décor by collectors; this scene features a medallion of two swans on a lake over a background of cobalt and gold. Known to exist on chocolate and tea sets, vases, urns, plaques, dresser sets, and cracker jars. Pieces carry the blue #52 mark.

36. Cobalt golden forest: A medallion of heavily gilded gold trees with gold-tone forest in the background is featured on these pieces. The background is cobalt with gold swags. Pieces that are known to exist with this decoration are vases and urns and carry the blue #52 mark.

37. Cobalt and gold scroll: A long time popular pattern among collectors, this décor is done in stunning cobalt with gold scroll along the top and bottom. Known to exist on chocolate sets, tea sets, demitasse sets, vases, dresser sets, humidors, cake sets, and dinner plates. This décor carries the green #52 mark or the green #47 mark.

38. Cobalt red mountain: Possibly one of the most beautiful scenes done in cobalt, this décor features a beautiful mountain and river scene on a cobalt background. Trim work is cobalt with heavy gold and green jewelling. Known to exist on vases, urns, plaques, and chocolate sets. Pieces carry the blue #52 mark.

33.

34.

35.

36.

37.

38.

39. Moriage jeweled owl: Décor consists of intricate decoration of an owl and tree branch executed in moriage. Found on numerous vase molds and humidors. Pieces are marked blue #52.

40. Traditional gray moriage dragon: Many different Nippon molds have been decorated with the gray moriage dragon, and they generally carry the green #47 mark.

41. Traditional moriage flying swans: With finely decorated moriage flying swans on a gray background, this décor generally carries the blue #52 mark. Known to exist on a wide range of molds including humidors, vases, and urns.

42. White woodland: Decorated with a gentle woodland scene in earth tones featuring white moriage trees in the foreground, this décor was done on a wide range of molds including vases, humidors, smoke sets, and plaques. Pieces generally carry the green or blue #47 mark.

43. Swans at sunset: Moriage swans flying through a brightly colored marsh at sunset grace this décor. This pattern was produced on vases, plaques, tankards, and mugs. These pieces generally carry the blue or green #52 mark.

44. Moriage palm tree and camel rider: Highly detailed moriage palm tree and camel rider are the main decoration on these pieces. Items carry the green #47 mark and are known to exist on vases, jugs, plaques, tankards, and mugs.

45. Seagulls in the waves: Seagulls frolic in the waves in this décor that was painted on humidors, vases, plaques, and urns. These pieces are generally marked blue or green #52.

40.

39.

41.

42.

43.

44.

45.

46. Moriage flower basket: A moriage flower basket filled with roses is the centerpiece of this décor. Known to exist on plaques (10" and 11") and chocolate and tea sets, these pieces carry the green #47 mark.

47. Moriage burnished copper: A highly detailed décor of jeweled moriage with gold and copper tone overlay, this décor is known to exist on chocolate and tea sets, vases, and cracker jars, and carries the green mark #47.

48. Cockatoo in pines: A beautifully painted white cockatoo prepares to fly while perched in a pine tree is the décor of this popular design. Known to exist on vases and plaques, this décor carries the blue #52 mark.

49. Enchanted moriage forest: One of the most intricate of all the moriage décors, it features a forest of moriage trees all done in high relief. At present, this décor has only been found on vases and carries the blue #52 mark.

50. Moriage winter cottage: Décor features a winter scene with cottage all done in white moriage. Only known to be executed on vases, chocolate sets, and tea sets, with the vases always being molded in relief. Pieces carry the green #47 mark.

46.

47.

48.

49.

50.

51.

52.

51. Moriage grapes with swans: Muted earth tones with two swans on a lake framed by moriage grapes and leaves are the main attraction on these pieces. Known to exist on vases, ewers, and plaques, pieces carry the blue #52 mark.

52. Moriage wrens: A colorful combination of painted and moriage wrens highlight these pieces. Further decorated by bands of spider-like enamel moriage treatment, these pieces are known to exist on various vase molds, humidors, and urns, and carry the blue #52 or green #47 marks.

53. Moriage lotus and cranes: A large moriage crane stalks among the moriage lotus leaves on this unusual décor. This decoration is only known to have been used on vases, and these are generally unmarked.

54. Christmas deer: This popular pattern featuring a stag's head surrounded by leaves and trees has been executed on numerous molds including tankard sets, humidors, jugs, and plaques. Pieces are marked green or blue #47.

55. Orange Gallé: Pieces show a river scene done in rich rust tones with moriage trees and heavy enameled bead and trim work. Known to exist on vases, jugs, plaques, smoke sets, humidors, chocolate sets, and cracker jars. Pieces carry the blue #52 or green #47 mark.

56. Burnished stoneware: This is an unusual décor done with low relief moriage featuring numerous floral and hoho bird treatments and then finished with a gold wash. Known to exist on ashtrays, vases, humidors, match holders, and trays. Pieces are marked green #47.

57. Lavender orchid Wedgwood: These pieces regardless of size are always breathtaking. Large lavender orchids in panels circle the piece and are trimmed top, bottom, and sides with a lavender background and white moriage overlay. Known to exist on vases, bowls, and compotes, pieces carry the green #47 mark.

58. Faux cloisonné: Done in a deco Oriental motif with Greek key border, this décor is found on various vase molds and carries the green #47 mark.

53.

54.

55.

59. Dutch dog walk: Done in stylized décor, these pieces feature a Dutch woman and boy walking a dog. This décor is found on numerous molds including vases, jugs, humidors, plaques, and dresser, smoke, and tea sets and carries the blue #47 mark.

56.

57.

58.

59.

60. **Red river:** High detailed, this décor depicts a peaceful stream flowing through a forest during fall. This décor has been found on vases, plaques, and humidors, and carries the green #47 mark.

61. **Shadows at the waterhole:** Done in rich vibrant primary colors, this décor features Indians and horses at sunset and is inspired by the work of artist Frederic Remington. This scene has been found on humidors and plaques, and pieces carry the green #47 mark.

62. **Midnight swan:** Beautifully painted scene of two swans swimming on a moonlit pond is found on vases, humidors, and plaques, and carries the green or blue #47 mark.

63. **Stylized barnyard:** Done in several variations, this décor features a barnyard scene with people. This decoration has been found on plaques, steins, humidors, and vases. Pieces carry the green #47 mark.

64. **Hidden door:** Featuring a mountain village done in primary colors, this scene is of interest due to the "hidden door" painted into the side of a mountain. Known to exist on plaques, humidors, vases, and cigarette boxes. Pieces carry the green #47 mark.

65. **Man in a boat:** Generally having highly decorative trim, these pieces depict a man preparing for boating. Known to exist on plaques and a number of vase molds, pieces carry the green #47 mark.

66. **Man on a horse:** Pieces feature a man watering his horse highlighted by trees in gold and a lavender tinted sky. Pieces are occasionally done with cobalt trim work. This décor can be found on urns, plaques, and vases, and carries the green #47 mark.

61.

60.

62.

63.

64.

67.

65.

66.

67. Oil spot: The prominent feature of these pieces is a dark gray background that appears to be stained with oil. Featuring heavy gold overlay, the décor is found on candlesticks, steins, vases, humidors, and various smoking piece, and carries the green #47 mark.

68. **Landseer's Newfoundland:** Featuring a painting of Landseer's Newfoundland; pieces are done in sepia tones and known to exist on humidors and plaques. Items carry the green #47 mark.

69. **Incised Indian:** Pieces are decorated with a stylized Indian done in earth tones and this decoration is known to exist on humidors, plaques, steins, and various smoking pieces. Items carry the green #47 mark.

70. **White hunt scene:** An intricate English hunt scene is the hallmark of these pieces. Known to exist on vases, jugs, tankard sets, humidors, and plaques. These pieces are marked with the green or blue #47 mark.

71. **Man on a cart:** With the feeling of an Old World painting, these pieces depict a man driving a cart near what appears to be a beach. Pieces are known to exist on two molds of vases and wall plaques and marked with the green #47 mark.

72. **Cow at water's edge:** This popular pattern features cows resting at the edge of a pond. Known to exist on vases, urns, cracker jars, and rectangular plaques. Items carry the green #47 mark.

73. **Palette roses:** A medallion of roses is featured on a field of matte green with gold overlay on these Victorian influenced pieces. This décor is known to exist on chocolate and tea sets, cracker jars, urns, vases, and serving trays. Pieces carry the blue #52 mark.

74. **Jeweled orchid:** Possibly one of the best painted and most sought after of the floral décors, this pattern has been found on urns, chocolate and tea sets, dresser sets, and vases, and carries the green #47 mark.

69.

68.

70.

71.

72.

73.

74.

75. Traditional Halloween: Featuring a stylized village done in primary colors, this pattern is seen both in matte glaze pieces and tapestry. Found on ewers, plaques, humidors, and a wide number of vases. Pieces carry the blue #52 mark.

76. Arrival of the coach: Highly intricate and stylized scene of an English coach is the main draw of these pieces. Known to exist on vases, jugs, and plaques, these pieces carry the green #47 mark.

77. Gouda: With the Dutch influence of Gouda ware, this decoration can be found on vases, humidors, candlesticks, chamber sticks, bowls, and various smoking items. These pieces carry the green #47 mark.

78. Man's best friend: This décor is of an old man in repose with a white dog. Pieces found with this decoration are vases, humidors, and plaques, and carry the green #47 mark.

79. Traditional hoho bird: A stylized hoho bird is the main feature on these pieces. It is found primarily on desk sets and smoke set pieces. Items carry the green #47 mark.

80. Playing card décor: Features various playing card décors. This decoration is generally found on humidors, smoke sets, mugs, and plaques. Pieces carry the green #47 mark.

81. New England winter: Décor depicts a barn in a snowy countryside and exists on vases and plaques. A relatively rare scene, on occasion décor will have silver overlay trees. Pieces are marked green #47 or RC when silver overlay is used.

75.

76.

77.

78.

79.

80.

81.

82. Clipper ship: A beautifully painted scene of clipper ships at sea, this décor is found on a wide range of molds. This decoration has been found on vases, urns, plaques (both round and rectangular), humidors, chocolate and tea sets, and candlesticks. Pieces carry the green #47 mark.

83. Man on a camel: This is an extremely popular décor featuring an Arab on camelback returning to his desert tent. Produced on a large number of molds including vases, urns, plaques (both round and rectangular), candlesticks, jugs, smoking pieces, chocolate sets, and tea sets. Pieces are marked with green #47.

84. Cleopatra's barge: Scene features an Egyptian barge and appears on plaques (both round and rectangular), vases, urns, smoking sets, and jugs. Pieces are decorated with various trim works and carry the green #47 or blue #52 mark.

85. Green hunt scene: With a stylized hunt scene and light moriage treatment over a field of green, this decoration is found on plaques, jugs, tea and chocolate sets, humidors, and dresser sets. Pieces are marked blue #52.

86. Coming to the call: This décor is growing in popularity and features an Indian at dusk riding in a canoe. The artist, Frederic Remington, originally painted this scene. It features both a plain and geometric border and is found on plaques, humidors, vases, and various utilitarian items. Pieces carry the green #47 mark.

87. Texas rose: Lavishly adorned with big plushy cream and rust tone roses, this décor is found on humidors, various molds of vases, urns, and chocolate and tea sets. Pieces are marked #52.

82.

83.

84.

85.

86.

87.

88. **Floral swirl:** Over a background of mottled yellow and magenta swirls, lovely roses or mums adorn this pattern in combination with heavy gold overlay. This pattern is found on vases, urns, and chocolate and tea sets, and they are marked with the blue #52 mark.

89. **Midnight windmill:** Depicting a Dutch windmill scene on a moonlit night, this décor carries the green #47 or blue #52 mark and can be found on humidors, chocolate and tea sets, vases, urns, and plaques.

90. **Dark woodland:** Featuring a stylized woodland scene, this décor was produced on a wide range of molds including tankard sets, smoke sets, chocolate and tea sets, jugs, dresser sets, humidors, plaques, urns, vases, and a wide assortment of utilitarian pieces. Items are found with the green #47 or blue #52 mark.

91. **Haunted lagoon:** This scene depicts a pond or swamp scene with enameled green and blue trees in the foreground. Carrying the green #47 mark, this décor has been found on vases and plaques.

92. **Knights at war:** Featuring a highly stylized décor of two knights going to battle, this scene is known to exist only on vases and humidors, and carries the green #47 mark.

93. **Satin Rookwood:** This décor features a version of a Rookwood décor with earth tone irises on a satin bisque finish. Carrying the Kinran #88 mark, this decoration is known to exist on vases and tankards.

89.

88.

90.

94. Glossy Rookwood: This décor features a version of Rookwood décor with earth tones, irises, and a glossy finish. Pieces carry the blue #52 mark. This decoration is found on chocolate sets, plaques, and vases.

91.

92.

93.

94.

95. Pink enamel swirl: Depicting a gentle floral motif over a field of pink and yellow mottled swirls, this décor can be found on vases, chocolate and tea sets, and cracker jars. Pieces are marked with the green #52 mark.

96. Kneeling pharaohs: This brightly colored décor features various Egyptian hieroglyphics and kneeling pharaohs. The décor is known to exist on candlesticks, vases, bowls, desk items, and jugs, and carries the green #47 mark.

97. Cypress by the lake: Featuring a house and lake scene, this décor has a stand of cypress in the foreground executed in green and rust tone enamels. This décor is found on plaques, vases, and humidors, and carries the green #47 mark.

98. Aqua flying swan: Trimmed in heavy gold and enameled jewelling, the hallmark of these pieces is swans flying through marsh reeds. Known to exist on a variety of molds including chocolate and tea sets, vases, dresser sets, ferners, candlesticks, and urns. Pieces are marked blue or green #52 and blue or green #47.

99. Airplane décor: A somewhat primitive scene, this décor features an old biplane and is known to exist on plaques, smoking set pieces, tea tiles, small vases, and numerous other small utilitarian pieces. Items are marked green #47.

100. Island waves: Waves rush to shore on this beautifully painted pastel décor. This décor is found on humidors, chocolate and tea sets, and vases. Pieces are marked green #47.

95.

96.

97.

98.

99.

100.

101. Dancing peasants: A stylized group of peasants standing on a beach with a blue and gray marbleized background are the main feature of these pieces. Pieces known to exist with this decoration are steins, humidors, and various vase molds. Items are marked with the blue #47 mark.

102. Captive horse: This décor features two dogs and a horse communing. These stylized pieces are generally trimmed with some type of heavy clay moriage, and this decoration is known to exist on plaques (round and rectangular), inkwells, and humidors. Pieces are marked green #47.

103. Molded Indian on horseback: Depicting an Indian on horseback riding into battle, this décor is most often found on 10" plaques, but is occasionally seen on chargers, ferners, and humidors. Pieces are marked green #47.

104. The fisherman: This is a rare molded décor and known to exist on jugs, humidors, vases, tankard sets, and rectangular plaques. The items are marked green #47.

105. Molded Egyptian: This rare molded décor is found on various desk set pieces, humidors, cigarette boxes, and candlesticks, and these items are marked green #47.

106. Mountainside brambles: This molded décor resembles the side of a mountain and has fall colored brambles as accent. Pieces are marked green #47.

101.

102.

103.

104.

105.

106.

Manufactured in Japan,
Hand Painted in the United States

Collectors have known for quite a while that most items backstamped Noritake/Nippon, #68, were once "in the white" blanks exported from Japan for decoration in the United States. The Pickard Co. as well as some of the smaller decorating studios such as Jonroth, Spicer Studios, Kenilworth, etc. used these wares. The Pickard Co. decorated many of these items in what is referred to as a gold etched design. According to the company this was done not because the china was of poor quality but to create an embossed look on these wares. Pickard also had their artists paint designs on other pieces.

Recently, I discovered that some rising sun and red M in wreath marked articles may also have been imported as "in the white" blanks. Many pieces of a dinnerware set were found in an atypical Noritake Co. decoration style. Parts of the set were marked Noritake/Nippon and some were the rising sun.

Part of a dinnerware set, bowl backstamped #68.

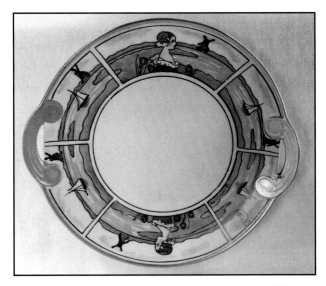

Pickard decorated cake plate, backstamped #68 and #76.

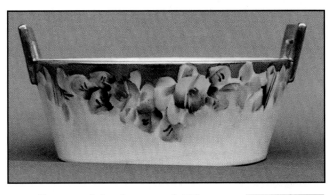

Butter tub backstamped #68.

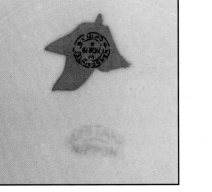

Cup and saucer, backstamp #84, rising sun mark.

The Noritake rising sun mark is usually found on utilitarian type wares that have a minimum of decoration. Previously, it was believed that all items marked with the rising sun backstamp were decorated in Japan but this could be new proof that this may not be the case. The small plate featuring seven mice as its decoration has the initials MGL written on the left side of the branch and does not look anything like pieces decorated in Japan.

China painting in the United States was very popular during the late 1800s and into the early 1900s. Many companies advertised china painting kits and blank pieces of porcelain for sale. Amateur artists painted these "in the white" items for personal use, to give as gifts, or for sale. Decorating studios all over the country also had their artists paint these blanks.

One dinnerware set has been found where the items were backstamped with three different marks. All pieces have the same design painted on them but some are marked with the red M in wreath, others KPM Silesia, and the remainder Thomas/Bavaria.

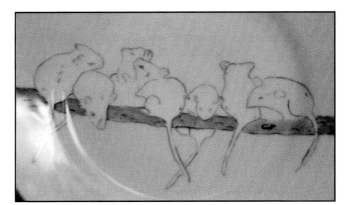

Small plate (rising sun mark) has initals MGL on right side of branch.

Old ads for instruction books and designs for china painting.

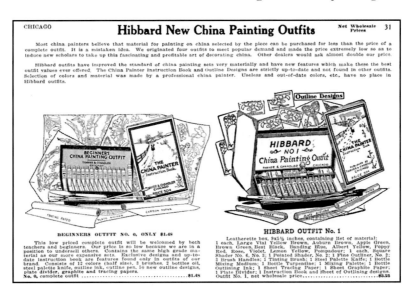

A tea set decorated with violets was found bearing the red M in wreath mark. Evidently someone named Lewis was the decorator and this is marked on the pieces. All the items appear to have been painted in the United States, as they are not typical of Japanese painted wares.

The more items we see the more puzzling things become. Are these pieces what we consider Nippon wares? We know that they were manufactured in Japan but most likely decorated in the United States. Many collectors do not consider them to be legitimate pieces of Nippon. Personally, I prefer the items manufactured and decorated by the Noritake Co. and its forerunner, the Morimura Brothers. But with these items, it is individual taste that counts, so you must be the judge.

Violet pattern teapot, sugar bowl, and creamer, 5c/s, artist signed "Lewis," red M in wreath hand painted Noritake Japan.

Many collectors enjoy finding items that have matching designs or portraits that are featured on Nippon pieces. They pair their porcelain pieces with matching old framed prints, jewelry, dresser items such as mirrors and brushes, tape measurers, pocket mirrors, and other types of ware such as Sevres and R.S. Prussia bearing the same decoration.

The wonderful molded in relief wall plaque shown in Photo 1 has been copied from N.C. Wyeth's painting entitled *The Hunter*, circa 1906. The original is presently displayed at the Brandywine River Museum at Chadds Ford, Pennsylvania. Inexpensive prints of this oil on canvas were popular during the Nippon era as well, see Photo 2. Collectors are beginning to decorate their homes with matching items and looking for these pieces has increased their collecting field.

Jewelry featuring many of the European beauties found on Nippon wares is also desirable, see Photo 3. The faces are either decals or hand painted on porcelain. A good magnifying glass can help the collector determine which is which. A decal, when viewed under a magnifying glass will have tiny dots making up the design. Hand-painted portraits generally cost more than the decal decorated ones. Most often the backing is good quality gold and

these items if old and in good condition sell for $100.00 to $250.00.

Celluloid pieces that match, such as the tape measure and pocket mirror shown in Photo 3 are also in demand. Celluloid boxes and photo albums are sometimes decorated with the same portrait or scene as found on Nippon wares. Other jewelry featuring Queen Louise is shown in Photo 4.

Many Nippon wall plaques, plates, and vases also feature some of these same beautiful women. The portrait wall plaque shown in Photo 5 can be found having either a cobalt or green border. Although the lady cannot be identified, the same decal was evidently popular and also used on a dresser set, see photo 6.

Jean François Millet's painting of *The Gleaners* is world famous and reproductions hung on walls across the United States and Europe in the 1880s, up to the 1920s and 1930s. Millet grew up in a Normandy hamlet of France and tilled, sowed, reaped, and cared for farm animals with his great-uncle and father on their farm. He glorified the peasant in his paintings most likely due to his upbringing. This experience enabled him to apply

Photo 1

Photo 2

Photo 3
Top row, left to right: Pin featuring Lebrun, pin featuring Potocka, pin featuring Queen Louise, pin featuring Queen Louise.
Bottom row, left to right: Pin featuring Lebrun, celluloid tape measure featuring Queen Louise, celluloid advertising pocket mirror featuring Queen Louise, pin featuring Queen Louise.

Photo 4
Necklace and pin featuring Queen Louise.

Photo 6

Photo 5

his academic training with particular veracity. After the European revolution of 1848 most peasants were regarded as brutes, and the bourgeois considered much of Millet's work confrontational and savage when he first started painting. He was an Impressionist painter and said to be the founder of Realism.

The Gleaners features three women in headscarves gathering the remnants of the wheat harvest. One version of this painting is found in the form of a decal that was placed on the large Nippon vase shown in Photo 7. Matching items featuring this scene abound. Collectors have found framed prints, circular medallions (also known as flue covers), and numerous celluloid items bearing this decoration, see Photo 8.

Old Butler Bros. Catalog ads from 1907 to 1916 show that this particular scene was placed on all kinds of wares during this time period, as seen on next page.

A wonderful hand-painted Sevres tea set features four women, Marie Louise, Josephine, Reine Hortense, and Recamier, see Photo 9. A close-up view of a younger Josephine is shown in Photo 10, and a close-up of the teacup featuring a hand-painted version of Madame Recamier is shown in Photo 11.

The cobalt R.S. Prussia celery dish in Photo 12 has four portrait medallions of three different women, Lebrun, 13; Potocka, 14; and Recamier, 15. These three beauties are also found on many Nippon items.

The hairbrush shown in Photo 16 and the porcelain mirror in Photo 17 are both parts of dresser sets and feature Madame Recamier as their decoration.

In Photo 18, the framed print is of Anna Potocka, also known as Sophie Potozki. A small, framed print on porcelain of Anna Potocka is in Photo 19.

Readers should refer to the portrait chapter of this book for more information on these portraits.

Photo 7

Photo 8
Top row: Framed print, celluloid sewing box.
Bottom row: Circular medallion (flue cover), celluloid autograph box.

Photo 9

Photo 10

Photo 11

Photo 12

Photo 13 – Lebrun

Photo 14 – Potocka

Photo 15 – Recamier

Photo 16

Photo 17

Photo 18

Photo 19

The prices of items featuring portraits on them are skyrocketing, especially those surrounded with coralene decoration or having a cobalt background. Almost every portrait featured on a Nippon piece is a decal (short for the word *decalcomania*). Decals are also referred to as transfer prints, and the use of decals was very popular during the Victorian and Edwardian periods. The decalcomanias used on Nippon wares were obtained in Europe because it was felt that the Japanese artist would have a predilection to give Japanese features to the faces.

Decalcomanias were also called penny transfers, and today they are found on all sorts of items. Sheets of decals were often made up of repeating separable transfers. The lithography used was very suggestive of the chromolithography techniques and of other complex lithography of the period.

A study of the backstamps found on Nippon portrait pieces indicates that approximately 85% bear the maple leaf mark (1891 – 1911), 10% have the M in wreath backstamp, and 5% are either unmarked or bear other various marks. This indicates to collectors that the Noritake Company or its forerunner, Morimura Brothers manufactured the majority of the portrait pieces.

Popular portraits featured are Madame Lebrun, Queen Louise, Madame Recamier, Marie Antoinette, Marie de Medicis, Empress Josephine de Beauharnais, Countess Anna Potocka (who may also be identified as Countess Sophie Potozki), lady with doves, lady with peacock, the Cardinal, and some of the Four Seasons ladies.

The majority, however, are presently unidentifiable, and at times one must consider that they are just pretty women with no nobility attachment and may just be the artist's wife or friend. The headgear on some indicates that a few may be Russian women. When identifying the women, the clothing and hairstyle are quite helpful. For example, the French women always bared their bosom as opposed to the English who wore buttons up to or covering the neck. The German ladies were usually more buxom than the French.

Two poses are found of Madame Recamier (1777 – 1849), see Photos 1 and 2. Her maiden name was Jeanne Julie Adelaide Bernard, and she was described as a brazen beauty by Napoleon. One pose

shown is from the portrait drawn by J. Champagne which he adapted from the original painting by Francois Pascal Simon Gerard. A copy of Champagne's drawing was found in an old 1800s book and is shown in Photo 3.

Madame Recamier was a native of Lyons, and she was usually called Juliet. In 1793, at the age of 16, she married a banker by the name of Recamier. By the time she was 27, she was regarded as the most beautiful woman in Europe. She was pro-

Photo 1

Photo 2

Photo 3

claimed an unrivaled beauty, her face so childish and yet so blooming, so lovely, and so very beautiful. Her smile was said to be gracious, the expression of her eyes was mild and intellectual, her language fascinating, and she was full of grace, goodness, and intelligence. It was also said that when men set eyes upon her she became an object of desire, yet her virtue remained pure, and her unsullied reputation never suffered from attacks of jealousy or envy. However, Napoleon's jealousy of Madame Recamier's beauty and influence and particularly her virtue brought about her exile from Paris. Napoleon exiled her because she refused to be his mistress, and when her husband's banking business was in trouble, he wouldn't help them. Her home had become the meeting place of many political meetings, and she was considered to be a reformer of morals and a renovator of society.

Vigee-Lebrun always regretted that she never had the opportunity to paint her, but she did comment that Madame Recamier was truly a beautiful lady. The Recamier couch, a long reclining one like the one she posed on for her famous portrait, is named after her.

Queen Louise is also featured in two poses — one is of just her head (Photos 4 and 5). Most people did not know that she wore a scarf around her throat because she wanted to conceal the fact that she had a goiter. (This was before the day of goiter surgery.)

Photo 4   Photo 5

She was born Louise of Meckinburg-Strelitz in 1793, and when she was only 17, she captured the heart of Frederick William III, heir to the throne of Prussia. When Madame Lebrun first saw her in

1801, she was dumb struck by her beauty and her heavenly face. Napoleon felt that Queen Louise had a pretty face but little intelligence and quite incapable of foreseeing the consequences of what she did. Her people considered her a heroine and her patriotic bearing in the Napoleonic Wars won her great popularity. In 1807, she humiliated herself at Tilsit before Napoleon, begging him to lighten the peace terms of Prussia.

She was described by some as an exquisite and fragile butterfly having a gift of beauty as great as that of a Greek statue. Paintings of her show long, jet black hair, a whiteness of complexion, and clingy Grecian-styled clothing of contemporary fashion. She gave birth to nine children in 14 years, the last less than a year before her death.

Countess Anna Potocka (Photo 6) has been described as a Polish lady and was married to her third husband when Madame Vigee-Lebrun painted her portrait. According to records, she confided to

Photo 6

Vigee that she was going to take her first husband back although he was a drunkard! Very few people realize that at times the Catholic Church did not frown on divorce but allowed it. This is why she had been married three times and was still in favor with the Catholic Church.

A twist to this story, however, was discovered lately when an old copy of *The Aldine* published in New York in 1873 was found. This article shows a picture of a lady who collectors have been referring to as Countess Potocka but with a much different story. This one tells us that she was born in Greece in 1773 to a poor shoemaker and his wife. She was considered a beauty, and in 1786, the Marquis de Beauviere purchased Sophie for the sum of 1,500 piastres. Three years later, she met and fell in love with the Russian Count and General Johann Dewitt who then purchased her from her first husband. Later, she met Count Stanislaus Felix Potozki who was fabulously wealthy, and he paid DeWitt an enormous sum to release Sophie so that he too could marry her. He died in 1803 and left Sophie a widow until her death in 1823. The picture shown in *The Aldine* is definitely that of our known Anna Potocka, and the similarity of three marriages is also discussed. Can Anna Potocka really be Sophie Potozki? Readers will have to read *The Aldine* (page 107) article and decide for themselves.

Two self-portraits are found of Madame Lebrun on Nippon wares. One is of her wearing a white ribbon in her hair (Photo 7), and the other one shows her wearing a white cap and a white ruffle around her neck (Photo 8). Madame Marie Louise Elisabeth Vigee-Lebrun was born on April 16, 1755, and died March 3, 1842.

Photo 7   Photo 8

Madame Lebrun was a French portrait painter who was trained by her father, Louis Vigee, who was also a painter. She painted Queen Marie Antoinette and her children, and many of these paintings are now in the Versailles museum. She was a painter of royalty until her death, and most of her portraits were of pretty women shown in fine feminine costumes of the period. She was one of the foremost painters of her era, and she received official and critical recognition during this period.

She was the official portraitist for Marie Antoinette and painted at least 25 portraits of her in her lifetime. In *Memoirs of Madame Vigee-Lebrun*, she comments on how she had to shade the thick Austrian lips of Marie Antoinette and how she had to make her nose appear more feminine.

She also painted about 25 self-portraits, two copies of which are found on Nippon pieces. Lebrun also painted *Peace Bringing Back Plenty*, and eight of her paintings are featured in the Louvre. She was admitted to the Royal Academy when she was only 23 years old.

She was married to Jean Baptiste Pierre Lebrun, but this marriage resulted in a sad life for her. Her husband used all the money she made painting to gamble. Later in life, her daughter left her, and she had to be taken care of by a niece in her last years.

There are also two portraits featured on Nippon pieces of Marie Antoinette (1755 – 1793), Photos 9 and 10. Marie Antoinette was Queen of France, wife of King Louis XVI. Her father was the Austrian Emperor, and she grew up very spoiled. She was said to be scarcely educated. She was neither loved nor respected by the French people, instead she was the object of hatred for her self-indulgence. She didn't understand the common people, and they detested her. She eventually fell victim to the Reign of Terror.

Marie de Medici, Photo 11, was the daughter of Francesco de Medici, grand duke of Tuscany and the queen of France. She became the second wife of

Photo 9   Photo 10

Photo 11

A LIFE'S ROMANCE.

IN the second half of the last century there lived in the Greek quarter of Constantinople a poor shoemaker, who had nothing he could call his own except a large and growing family. His children were remarkable for beauty, the pure Grecian type being developed in each one to a degree that excited universal wonder. The eldest, a girl born in 1773, was considered the most beautiful child in the whole city; and the poor shoemaker's friends used to say that Sophie, for that was her name, would yet make his fortune.

But how? By winning a wealthy son-in-law? Yes, but not exactly in the fashion which we are used to. At that time — and it is still the case to a great extent — the possession of a beautiful daughter was too often the means of enriching a poor man in a manner which Christian people regard with horror and detestation. Under the shameful code of morals then prevalent in the Turkish capital, the trade in beautiful women was not considered dishonorable. Greek girls as well as Circassian were sold in the public market, and the man who refused to accept a good price for a beautiful daughter, was regarded as overscrupulous, or a fool.

In 1786, the old Marquis de Beauviére, French ambassador at the court of the Sublime Porte, saw the shoemaker's beautiful daughter, and was so captivated by her charms that he bought her of her father for the sum of 1,500 piastres. His bargain was soon concluded. The poor shoemaker was raised above necessity, and no one ever thought of asking the daughter's consent. She was at once transferred to the ambassador's palace, and there surrounded with all the luxuries and delights that wealth could bestow. She was richly clothed, attended by crowds of obsequious servants, learned to speak and write French, and attained considerable proficiency in music and other polite accomplishments.

Three years passed in this bewildering whirl, when the marquis was summoned back to France. He decided, for various reasons, to pursue the land route through Poland and Russia. It was his intention to transplant his beautiful Greek captive to his estate in the south of France, there being many reasons for not taking her to Paris. Stopping to rest a few days at the Russian frontier fortress of Kaminiezk-Podolsk, he inconsiderately allowed Sophie to accompany him on a visit to the commander of the post, Count Johann De Witt, a handsome cavalier and man of the world, who had scarcely passed his thirty-third year. The contrast between him and the old marquis, who had kept her jealously from the sight of younger men, made a powerful impression on the susceptible heart of the young girl. The commandant was equally impressed; and the natural result followed. He found means to declare his love, and was assured that it was returned. It only remained to get rid of the ambassador on some reasonable pretext. Under pretense of viewing the beauties of the country, he was induced to accompany an adjutant in a ride outside the walls, leaving Sophie in charge of a lady. No sooner was he outside than the gates were closed. De Witt took the beautiful Greek before the priest, who speedily married them. The commandant was above small meanness. He met the enraged marquis at the gate, paid him over the exact sum he had given for Sophie, and then, in the most polite manner, and with many wishes for his safe journey home, dismissed him.

In this way the poor shoemaker's daughter, the most beautiful woman of the century, became the wife of the Russian General De Witt, and entered upon still another phase of life. But it soon became evident to both that somehow a mistake had been made. Their feeling for each other proved to be a transient passion. A child was born to them, but it did not make their union more loving. Sophie grew tired of the monotonous life of a small frontier town, and longed to visit St. Petersburg, of whose festivities and luxuries glowing accounts reached her from time to time.

With many misgivings De Witt at length yielded to her importunities; St. Petersburg at that time surpassed even Versailles in the luxury and frivolity of court life. Sophie burst upon this life like a new-risen star. Her beauty dazzled every eye. Even Catherine, in her declining years as great a sinner as in her youth, and subject to frightful paroxysms of jealousy when her lovers were attracted by younger charms, could not repress her admiration for this beautiful apparition from the south. The proudest nobles hastened to lay their wealth and titles at her feet. Among them was Count Stanislaus Felix Potozki, who was reckoned the handsomest, as he was among the richest, of all the courtiers who gave eclat to the voluptuous court of Catherine. He was in the very prime of life, an aristocrat born and bred; a field marshal of distinguished services, and a great favorite with the empress. General De Witt's misgivings about introducing his beautiful wife into the whirl of court life were only too well founded. Sophie and Count Potozki fell in love at first sight. It is said they came to an understanding the first evening they met, at a court ball. There were barriers in the way which prevented a repetition of the play at the garrison town. Sophie was now the wife of a Russian general. But she had been bought once; why not again? Potozki was very rich. On his vast estates were above 200,000 serfs. He made the offer of an enormous sum to De Witt, conditioned on his releasing Sophie; and the general, knowing that he should lose her, concluded to make the best of a bad matter. The bargain was soon concluded. Sophie was divorced from De Witt and immediately married to Potozki.

Catherine was incensed at the affair. No moral sense was left to be offended, but her vanity was deeply wounded, and certain plans for Potozki's political preferment, on which she had set her heart, were irrevocably deranged. The count retired to his estates with his beautiful wife, and there remained in retirement until the death of the empress. But the countess, her heart at rest, had learned to love retirement. She passed much of her time on a beautiful estate in the Crimea, on which Potozki had expended fabulous sums of money. Here two sons were born to them; and here, in 1803, Potozki died. The countess, still beautiful, occasionally appeared at court afterward, but for the most part lived on her estates, devotedly loved by friends and dependents for her kindness and benevolence. She died of consumption, in 1823, at Berlin, where she had gone to seek medical advice.

THE COUNTESS POTOZKI.

Henry IV in 1600 and was regent for her son, Louis XIII, after Henry's assassination in 1610.

Marie (1573 – 1642) was described as not pretty, having a face that was too full, scanty eyebrows, and an expressionless mouth. It is said that in later life, she showed herself to be both obstinate and dull. Rubens painted her portrait, and these paintings hung in her Luxembourg palace.

Marie was also the mother of Queen Henrietta Maria of England. She dissipated the French treasury and was banished in 1617. Finally in 1631, she fled to the Netherlands, never to return.

Josephine de Beauharnais was one of the reigning queens of Parisian society (Photo 12). She was born in 1763 on the island of Martinique. She married Vicomte Alexandre de Beauharnais at the age of 16 and became Vicomtesse. During her marriage

Photo 12

to Alexandre, she gave birth to a son, Eugene, and a daughter, Hortense. Alexandre was executed in 1794, and Josephine met General Bonaparte when she was a widowed socialite living in Paris. They married but she didn't produce an heir for Napoleon, and they were subsequently divorced in 1809. A few weeks later, the Archbishop of Paris granted an annulment.

She was known for her elaborate dresses that were festooned with trinkets and jewels. During this time period, she often wore her hair a la guillotine which was a term for wearing one's hair pinned up to expose the neck. It is said that she had an uncontrollable passion for beautiful things, and she bought most things without even asking the price. She was a recklessly extravagant woman, and in 1809, she had 1,000 dresses in her wardrobe. She had purchased 500 pairs of shoes that year added to the 250 pairs she had bought the year before.

Josephine led an extremely luxurious life. She devoted herself to her appearance, spending three hours every morning bathing, getting dressed, and groomed. She changed her clothes three times a day. She enjoyed her amusements at court and was also interested in the cultivation of her gardens at Malmaison.

When she became Empress in 1804, she was said to be the perfect wife for Napoleon. She was boundlessly sympathetic, long suffering, and sweet-tempered, but it was essential that she produce an heir for him which she didn't do.

J. Champagne also drew Josephine's portrait as well as Madame Recamier's portrait. It is a version of this pose that was used on some of the Nippon wares (Photo 13).

Photo 13

The Cardinal is also featured on numerous Nippon items and is found in three poses. All three appear to be the same cardinal. This decal is often accompanied with moriage decoration and is desired by many collectors. Two of those poses are shown in Photos 14 and 15.

Cardinals are the highest dignitaries in the Roman Catholic Church after the pope and are considered ecclesiastical princes. They wear a scarlet colored robe and a distinctive red cap, or biretta, that is given to them by the pope. The College of Cardinals has existed since 1059 and has the duty of electing the pope.

Numerous other beautiful women including the so-called lady with doves (Photo 16) and lady with peacock (Photo 17) can also be found on Nippon porcelain items.

The archives of the Strong Museum Library in Rochester, New York, contain pages of old, sales catalogs featuring portrait decals from the German firm of C.S. Pocher, circa 1900 – 1915. Many of these decals look exactly like those used on some Nippon pieces.

The following photographs include many of the other unnamed beauties appearing on pieces of Nippon porcelain.

Photo 14

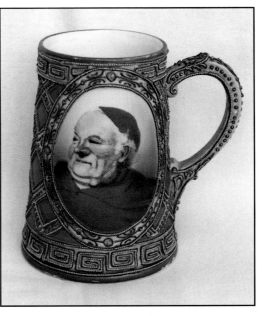

Photo 15

Photo 16

Photo 17

Other Popular Portraits

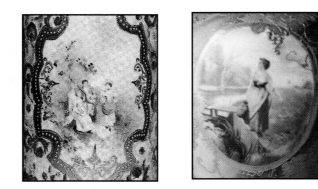

Just when you think you've seen almost everything that's ever been made in the Nippon era, some new and incredible pieces emerge. A few are rare; others are just highly unusual. Some tend to be expensive as well as highly desirable by most collectors. Others are just unusual to find and do not necessarily cost a lot of money. Then there are those I call fun pieces because they're somewhat bizarre.

The dictionary defines rare as scarce, extraordinary, exceptional, unique, seldom found, and few and far between. Unusual is defined as not common, odd, bizarre, and untypical. Some of the following pieces fall into both categories, but all are a reflection of the time period in which they were manufactured.

Two of the most rare and expensive items of Nippon to surface recently are the wall plaques shown in Photos 1 – 3. The wonderful molded-in-relief (blown-out) charger is 14" in diameter and is painted in strong, rich, vivid colors. This charger (a wall plaque that is 14" wide or larger) has a scene of two young children sitting under a tree. Collectors have also found a matching humidor and vase in this pattern, and the vase is shown in plate 1513. This is an incredible piece of Nippon.

Another unbelievable wall plaque is rectangular in shape, 10¼" x 8". Previously, collectors only knew of twelve hand-painted and two molded-in-relief designs painted on rectangular plaques, see page 60 of *Collector's Encyclopedia of Nippon Porcelain, Fifth*

Series. Then, this new design showed up and stunned the Nippon community. Like the others, this plaque is "framed" and is an exceptional piece of Nippon.

Photo 2

Photo 3

Photo 1

Photo 4 is a porcelain medallion that may have been used at the Morimura Brothers Store at 546 & 548 Broadway, New York City. The piece is small and measures 5⅜" high and 4" wide. Although not large in size, it is an incredible item to own. It's decorated in a floral pattern just as a small plate would be. It either was used at the store or perhaps was a giveaway. Either way, it's a sensational item.

Photos 5 – 12 are pieces that feature symbols of the Pacific Northwest. The tray in Photo 5 is almost 10" in diameter and bears the M in wreath mark. This design portrays Pacific Northwest Coastal Indian totem characters. Each of these characters has a specific role in storytelling and the legends of these Indians. Not only have collectors found this tray but a humidor and ashtray as well. So far only smoking items have been located.

Photos 6 – 10 show close-ups of these characters. Photo 6 is of a sea otter with a brown face and paws on its chest. Photo 7 is probably a flicker woodpecker. Photo 8 is a mythical Northwest Indian character, and Photo 9 features a raven which is the focal character of Northwest Coastal Indian lore. In Hilary Stewart's *Looking at Indian Art of the Northwest Coast*, she states that the raven is the most important of all creatures to the coastal Indian peoples. It was the raven, the transformer, the cultural hero, the

trickster, the Big Man (he took many forms to many peoples) who created the world. Photo 10 is a mythical character, possibly the moon.

A theory of why more Pacific Northwest Coastal Indian art on Nippon porcelain is not found may be because the wood totems were not made in the Seattle, Washington area, and there was little interest in totems in that area, at the time. Early missionaries tended to destroy or discourage the use of totems as they considered them deities. In fact, the totems were stories of the families's origins and accomplishments.

Another hindering fact was that the Japanese were unable to interpret and reproduce the characters to give them their full meaning. Most totem art pieces were done in a column rather than segmented. The colors used on the Nippon pieces are not traditional and specific colors for particular animals/items were extremely important in the traditional Pacific Northwest Coastal Indian pieces. The ashtray in photo 11 is 4½" wide, and the humidor shown in photo 12 is 7" tall.

The items in Photos 13 and 14 imitate Royal Bayreuth wares. The small mustard pot is shaped and decorated like a tomato. It is a copy of one of the designs that is popular on the Royal Bayreuth marked pieces. Collectors can refer to Plate 590 for

Photo 4

Photo 5

Photo 6

Photo 7

Photo 8

Photo 9

Photo 10

Photo 11

Photo 12

Photo 13

Photo 14

a tea set decorated in this particular pattern. I have not seen the molded corn design before, and the creamer is evidently part of a tea set. This is a very unique piece of Nippon, and both of these items carry the M in wreath mark.

Photos 15 and 16 are of an unusual compote. It is 8½" tall and bears the blue maple leaf backstamp. Having never seen this particular item in all my Nippon collecting years, I was shocked to then find two within a matter of one month. It's a truly unique piece.

Photos 17 and 18 are of a hanging toothbrush holder. This particular one is 4⅛" tall and has the green M in wreath mark. Very few collectors have ever seen one of these items and although its purpose was utilitarian, this particular piece was decorated with a very nice scenic decoration.

Photos 19 and 20 are of a small, cobalt and gold ferner. At first glance it looks like a small bowl but it is actually a two-piece ferner. The insert even has a drain hole in the bottom. An item such as this are extremely difficult to locate. It is 3¾" wide with a backstamp of green #4.

Photos 21 – 23 are of a wonderful ashtray. Could this have belonged to the father of Bessie, Tessie, and Essie? This is evidently a custom-signed piece, highly unusual, and the written names are definitely indicative of ones used during the Nippon era. The piece is 6¼" wide, 2½" tall, and is marked #47.

Photos 24 and 25 are of a nut bowl that would just be an ordinary piece except for the wonderful molded lion's head and feet. Without these, the piece would just be a run-of-the-mill item. The

piece carries the M in wreath mark and is superb because of these unique feet.

Photos 26 – 28 show a sensational manicure set. Although not marked, these items are definitely Nippon moriage decorated pieces. Any Nippon manicure set would be extremely rare to find, but this particular one is remarkable because it is in its original case. Occasionally, a collector will find the two-piece jars or a nail buffer but to find all of these items in their presentation box is fantastic.

Photo 29 is of a small plate painted with a decoration of seven mice sitting on a branch or log. Although this is not rare, it certainly is unusual. I believe that it was probably painted in the United States as the initials MGL are painted on the right side of the log.

Photo 30 is another unusual piece and one that I have not seen before with a Nippon backstamp. It is a 3" egg cup with its own individual salt and pepper and bears the TN mark #109.

Photo 31 is another view of the humidor shown in Plate 2618. It portrays Chief Red Cloud and is an absolutely spectacular item. What makes this one really different is that the cover of the humidor not only has a hole in it for a sponge, but it also has many other little holes surrounding it. This is unique for humidors.

Photo 32 is proba-

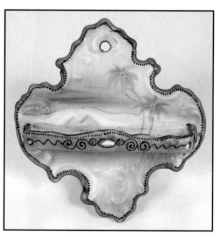

Photo 17

Photo 15

Photo 16

Photo 18

Photo 19

Photo 20

Photo 21

Photo 22

Photo 24

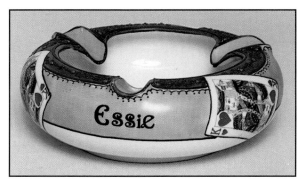

Photo 23

Photo 25

Photo 26

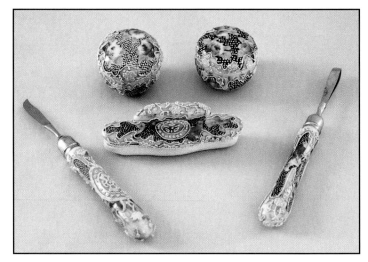

Photo 27

Photo 29

Photo 28

Photo 30

Photo 31

bly the most bizarre piece of Nippon I have ever encountered. It looks like an early lava lamp and is painted in the vivid colors of green and orange. It has the Royal Nishiki #91 backstamp along with the numbers 3695/4. Do the surprising pieces never end?

Photo 33 is an unusual vase although not an expensive piece. It has a double mouth at the top that is extremely unique to a bulbous vase.

Nippon continues to amaze and to educate. Evidently thousands of designs were painted on these wares, and we may never know about all of them. When the *First Series* was published, I felt that it was the definitive work on the subject. How wrong I was because here is the *Sixth Series* with the seventh following soon after and more new and wonderful items keep appearing each day. Happy hunting!

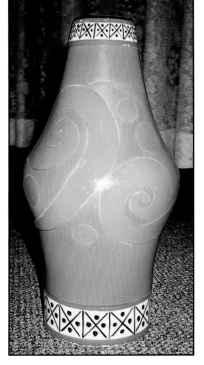

Photo 32

Photo 33

Motoring Scenes Featured on Nippon Porcelain

Collecting Nippon items decorated with motoring scenes can be a difficult task, and when such an item is found, it can be quite expensive. Motoring designs have been placed on all kinds of pieces such as humidors, spittoons, ashtrays, inkwells, desk sets or dresser trays, cups and saucers, nut dishes, and even children's tea sets. Most are found bearing the M in wreath mark or the rising sun backstamp that indicates that the Noritake Co. in Japan manufactured them after 1910.

A number of motoring enthusiasts look for early automobilia, and this extends to collecting porcelain items featuring old cars. Both groups of collectors are searching for these items, Nippon collectors and automobilia collectors.

It's difficult to imagine life without automobiles, but it really hasn't been that long since cars have been in use. Henry Ford built his first car in 1893, and by 1900 there were 8,000 autos in the United States. In 1903, Britain set the speed limit at 20 miles per hour in an attempt to control accidents!

Licensing was introduced in the United States around the turn of the century, although there were few restrictions. Prior to World War I, horseless carriages existed along with those pulled by horses, and by 1915 there were already 2.3 million automobiles in the United States.

Etiquette for Americans was a book published in 1910, and a chapter on motoring was included. The author identified herself only as "A Woman of Fashion." Excerpts from that book follow:

"Automobiles or motor cars at present so engross the attention of the modern world as to make it desirable to touch upon the etiquette of the situation. The sport has become so almost universal, however, it is in fact not much more than a question of carriages over motor cars again; yet the suggestion may be made that a man need not be a boor or look like a bear because he owns a motor car any more than if he rides in a carriage.

"The ordinary civilities need not disappear because one goes through space at thirty miles an hour instead of ten!

"A gentleman needs hardly to be warned against speaking always of his automobile any more than of his yacht!

"Both men and women should dress as quietly as possible in an automobile. In town, using one's car as a cab, one of course, dresses to the social exigencies of the moment, but on a tour some specialization may be necessary.

"A long skirt with high boots or leggings, an outing hat of some sort and quiet colors throughout distinguish the well-bred motoring lady. Small hats are best worn because they are more easily kept on. Covert cloth and tweed in gray, brown or dark blue or black are in good taste.

"Fancy hats with feathers or long quills are conspicuous, and to attract attention is the last thing a well-conducted automobilist desires. A distinctive device of motoring is the automobile veil, which secures the hat more confidently than pins.

"Black clothes get dusty sooner and show mud badly without a silk or linen duster. And for summer there has been revived, though in an altered aspect, the old linen duster of our grand-fathers. In winter all sorts of furs are called into requisition. Gauntlets add much to the comfort of man or woman on a long ride.

"In short, dress to be comfortable and to keep the wind out, a little ingenuity and good taste can accomplish this without one's looking a fright.

"Invitations to motor are informal from the nature of the sport, and may be of many pleas-ant kinds. Tea at a neighboring country place or club is one of the most popular raisons d'etre for a spin over good roads.

"A pleasant and neighborly, though now somewhat old-fashioned custom was to 'send a carriage for' one's friends, and this may be agree-ably revived with automobiles. The fortunate mistress of a motor car may discharge many social obligations by placing it at the disposal of a visiting friend from out of town.

"In England automobiles are called motors, a better name for them, and in America the ever short word 'car' is growing in vogue."

Most of the women featured on the "motoring" pieces wear special headwear as this was needed in an open car. Veils were not only decorative but also necessary to keep one's hat on. Veils also protected women from the cold and dust. Old ads referred to some of these hats as having dust-proof veils. Other ads showed hats that looked like a bag one placed over the head as it only had slits for the eyes! Thank goodness women no longer have to wear such tortu-ous outfits.

Inkwells, 2¾" square, 2¼" tall, mark #47.

Ladies spittoon, 3⅛" tall, 2½" wide, mark #47.

Desk set, 8¾" x 2¾", mark #47.

Child's tea set, rising sun mark #84.

Ashtray, 5½" wide, mark #47.

Cup and saucer featuring Geisha girls on transparent white china.

Close-up of ashtray.

Humidor, mark #47.

Humidor, mark #47.

The time period that items were backstamped with the word Nippon spanned from 1891 to 1921, the Gay Nineties to the Roaring Twenties. The porcelain reflected what was happening during that era not only with the various designs found but also with the numerous types of items that were manufactured.

The Victorian period historically ended in 1901, but its influence lasted until the outbreak of World War I in 1914. During this time, there was a compulsion to purchase, accumulate, and display possessions. Clutter was in and there was bric-a-brac everywhere.

In the Edwardian age, there was great ostentation and extravagance. Beginning in 1908 you could even purchase a home from Sears Roebuck. You just had to wait for the boxcar to arrive. It was possible to order a two-room cottage to a twelve-room residence.

Catalogs doubled as school aids. Children would practice their arithmetic by adding up orders, they could study geography from postal zone maps and all contained poetry and household tips. The Butler Brothers Company was a mail-order wholesaler to mainly country merchants and provided a wide range of items through their catalogs. Montgomery Ward and Sears Roebuck sold Nippon wares in their stores and through their catalogs.

In 1905, Sears began the Iowaization scheme. They sent two dozen catalogs to each Iowa customer and asked them to give the catalogs to friends and relatives. Then the customers were instructed to send in these names, which were monitored by Sears. Premiums were sent to those who got new customers for the company.

The Jewel Tea Company, Sperry and Hutchinson (S&H), and the Larkin Co. also gave premiums of Nippon wares to their customers. Nippon marked items were found everywhere.

In 1900, unskilled workers made an average of $8.37 a week and a girl of 12 – 13 tending a textile loom got $2.00 a week. By 1918, a woman working in a factory, six days a week made $1.50 a day. The average workweek in 1914 was 55 hours. Rent was $9.00 – $12.00 a month for the working class and food for a couple was $3.00 – $4.00 a week. In that same year, five cents could purchase three rolls or

donuts or an order of coffee and hotcakes or a quarter of a pie! However, when America entered World War I labor got a boost and so did wages.

In 1915 many rural families and city dwellers still had no running water. The kitchen usually held an icebox, as refrigerators only became available around the late 1910s. Coal stoves heated most homes and records show that over 7,000 models had been patented by 1919. But this required an hour a day just to shuttle the coal, tend the fire, and sift the ashes. Cleaning house took enormous time and effort. There usually was no electricity and no indoor plumbing. Dishwater, cooking slops, and chamber pots had to be taken outside. It's been estimated that the average housewife spent 27 hours a week cleaning her home.

Victorians took dining very seriously. In the grandest homes, elaborate dinners were served entirely by servants and the wealthy were helpless without their staff. In middle-class households, however, the residents had to do more work.

Dining etiquette required that conversation must be kept going but it was unheard of to chatter across the table. At the beginning of the meal, the hostess began conversing with the gentleman on her right, and the other ladies opened discussion with the gentlemen on their right. They talked through the first course and then, as the next course was served, the hostess began talking to the man on her left. All the other ladies followed suit. This was called "turning the table." At the end of the meal, the hostess put her napkin on the table, gathered up her gloves, looked at the other ladies, and stood up. The gentlemen stood as well and pulled back the chairs as the ladies filed from the table. The ladies clustered together in the ornate, feminine parlor while the men remained in the dining room. The tablecloth was removed, and decanters of wine and brandy were circulated — always clockwise as counterclockwise was considered bad luck. Dining in the Victorian era was never considered just eating. It was taken very seriously and many people suffered a great deal of anxiety about the manners required.

Dining etiquette manuals were published to instill a more aristocratic style of behavior, and etiquette has never strayed very far from its original intent: to protect rulers from contact with "lesser persons." (See illustrations below.)

Calling cards were part of proper etiquette during this time period. They were also called name cards or visiting cards and visitors were expected to furnish themselves with these cards. Though the ritual of paying calls was time consuming, it provided a system for forming and maintaining friendships. Women had what was called a "visiting list." And it was necessary to call on everyone at least twice a year. Of course, calls were made more often between closer friends, and it was always necessary to make calls in cases of illness, bereavement, or after being entertained by someone. These calls had to be returned, for a lack of reciprocity meant a resolution to discontinue the friendship!

On the visiting card, the address was usually placed under the name, towards the bottom of the card, and in smaller letters. Mourning cards were surmounted with a broad black margin about a ¼" in size, whereas half mourning only required a small black edge.

Calling cards were once the size of playing cards, but by the middle of the nineteenth century, the cards had shrunk to the dimensions of today's business cards.

In an old album of collected calling cards were the words "a left corner fold indicates that it's family, a right corner fold means a Mr. and Mrs., and no fold indicates that it is a single person."

The "call" consisted of a ceremonial visit lasting ten to fifteen minutes in length. The visiting lady did not even remove her hat or gloves; she merely perched on the edge of a chair with her purse on her lap. Both ladies made small talk and then the visitor would leave her card on the way out. There would be an appropriate receptacle for cards on the front hall table.

There were special rules for visiting as well. Visits of ceremony must be necessarily short. They were not to be made before the hour, nor yet during the time of luncheon. One should ascertain what the family hour for luncheon was and act accordingly. Evening visits were paid only to close friends, and morning visits should always be extremely brief.

One must always keep an account of one's visits and ladies were instructed to remember the intervals at which the visit was returned for it was necessary to let a similar interval elapse before a return visit was made. People in this way gave you notice whether they wished to see you often or seldom.

Gentlemen could simply put their calling cards into their pockets, but ladies usually carried them in a small elegant portfolio, called a card-case.

The telephone gradually replaced calling cards and today, calling card trays from the Nippon era are difficult to locate. (Photos on next page.)

Tea goes back so far that its true beginning has been lost in time. Chinese legend has it that in 2737 BCE, Emperor Shen Nung watched some small,

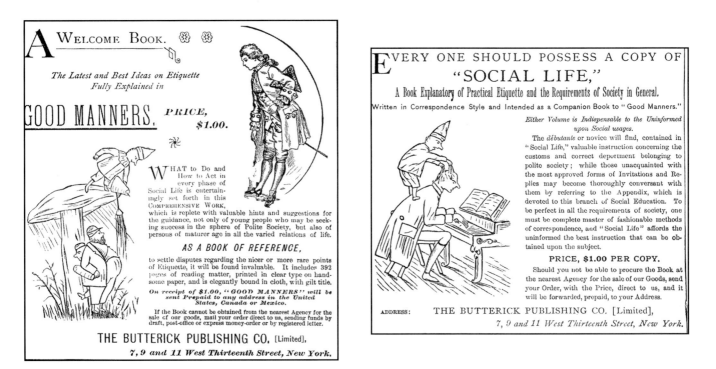

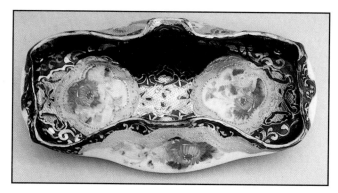
Calling card tray.

Victorian-era calling cards.

dry leaves flutter into a pot of boiling water that hung in his garden. He smelled the liquid, and decided that he liked it. He called it "cha" and from then on the beverage became part of his daily diet.

For years, the brewing of tea was unknown outside of China, but once the Far East could be reached by sea, traders discovered this beverage. Soon tea drinking became the rage all over Europe. There are three different types of tea — black, green, and oolong. They all come from the same tea bush, but it's what happens in the factory that makes them different.

Many people considered tea time in the Victorian era as a formal occasion complete with elegant silver, china, and dainty sandwiches. During this time, teabags did not exist and loose tea was used when preparing a cup of tea. To avoid getting tea leaves in the cup, a tea strainer was placed over the cup and

the tea was poured through it. The loose tea was caught in the strainer, and then the strainer was put back on the base to drip.

The following description was found in a book on manners written in 1891, "Tea and coffee should never be poured into a saucer. If a person wishes to be served with more tea or coffee, he should place his spoon in the saucer. If he has had sufficient, let it remain in the cup." So it seems that teacups were not the only things used for drinking tea, saucers were used as well!

A Ceramic Art Company catalog, circa 1900, listed many different types of "in the white" blanks for sale and among the items featured were tea strainers. An article entitled "Over the Teacups" told readers, "Have you poured tea? Then you know the sense of utter helplessness that comes when the cup is full and you have no place for the dripping strainer. We have met this difficulty by providing a drip-bowl large enough for every use, with a base so broad that it cannot tip over, and in such excellent proportion to the strainer that both together form a dainty table ornament. Besides its utility and beauty of design, this little article, indispensable on a well-equipped tea-table, has much in the quality of its fabric to recommend it to the amateur."

Tea strainer.

Collectors should always look for tea strainers that have both the strainer and the drip-bowl. Old ads for Nippon wares indicate that they were sold in this manner.

There were also special rules for home etiquette in the Victorian era, and many books were published on this subject. A lady's dressing room had to be furnished with a low dressing-bureau, a washstand, an easy chair placed in front of the dressing bureau, one or two other chairs, a sofa or couch if

Picture from home etiquette book.

Wash stand pictured in *Godey's Lady's Book*.

there is sufficient room, and a large wardrobe if there are not sufficient closet conveniences.

The dressing-bureau should contain the lady's dressing case, her jewel box, pincushion, ring stand, and hair pin cushion. There should also be a tray with various kinds of combs, frizettes, bottles of perfumes, etc.

Ladies were expected to brush their long hair twenty minutes in the morning, for ten minutes when it was dressed in the middle of the day, and for a like period at night. Women used hair receivers to store their hair after brushing or combing. In England, they are called "tidies," and this seems to be a good name for them as they tidied up the dressing area. As women cleaned their hairbrushes or combs, they tucked these combings into a two-piece hair receiver that had a lid with a circular hole. The collected hair was used for many purposes. Some was even knotted into jewelry.

This was also a period where infancy and childhood remained dangerous life stages, and many children succumbed at an early age. Pieces of hair were collected from a departed loved one and fashioned into a bracelet or necklace. These were worn to mark a period of mourning.

Victorians relished handicrafts and knotting and weaving hair was a popular pastime at that period in history. Hair wreaths were also made either with a living family member's hair or sometimes with a deceased relative's hair. Often times several family members' hair was used together.

Hairpieces or so-called "rats" were also made from these combings. Hair was added to a roll of wire mesh padding to make the rat. These monstrous hair-pads were placed on top of the head and held in place with the aid of hairpins and combs to give the hair fullness. Hair decorations were also made out of hair and placed in the hair for adornment.

This was a time when hats and bonnets were in fashion. No woman would think of going outside

Hair wreath in shadow box.

Hair receiver (above) and how it looks opened (right).

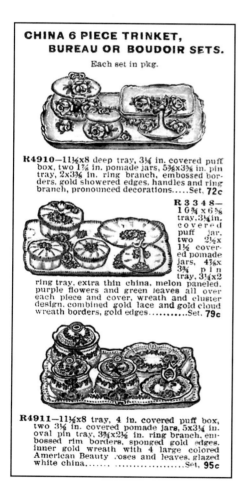
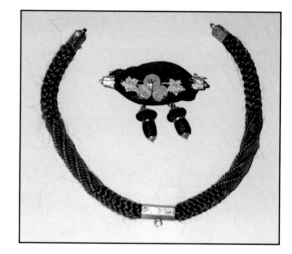

Hair jewelry.

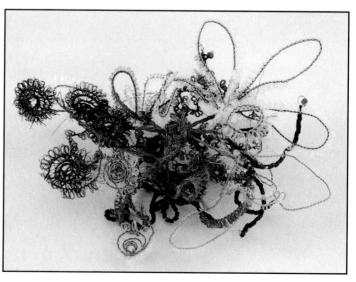

Hair decoration to be placed in hair.

without her hat, and in fact some women even wore hats in the house! Many of the fashionable hats of this time period were often huge in size and covered with flowers and/or feathers. During the Gay Nineties hats had become so bizarre that it's easy to imagine that the milliners were most likely laughing behind their customers' back.

Hats were secured with long elaborate hatpins that were necessary to skewer the hat to the coiffure. These could also be used as lethal weapons if needed, and laws were actually passed in some states banning them. Hatpin holders were invented to solve the problem of how to store the hatpins. Some were a three-in-one item (hatpin holder, pin tray, and ring tree), some just for hatpins and/or pins, and some could even be hung on the wall.

Hairpins were another necessity and hair pin cabinets and holders were placed on a lady's dressing table. Some hair pins were described as "invisible," while others could be found in colors. Nippon hair pin holders are extremely difficult to find and quite expensive considering their size.

Vanity organizers.

Victorian-era hat and hatpin.

Hairpin holder, closed and open.

WIRE HAIR PIN CABINETS.

1 doz. in carton.

N480 — 50 count, turned wood, plaid paper covered, asstd. straight and crimped. Doz. **24c**

N431 — 100 count, paper covered box, asstd. pins. Doz. **32c**

N433 — 50 count. polished wood box, asstd. colors, asstd. pins. Doz. **33c**

N504 — 100 count, 4 compartment cabinet silkaline paper covered. asstd. lengths invisible pins. Doz. **36c**

Old ads for hair pin cabinets and hair pins.

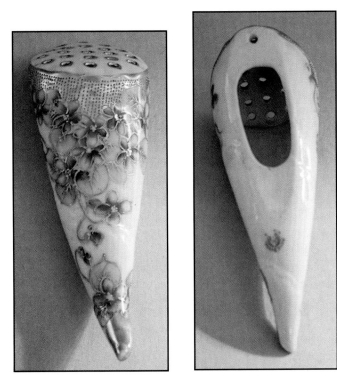

Hanging hatpin holder, front and back.

Dresser set.

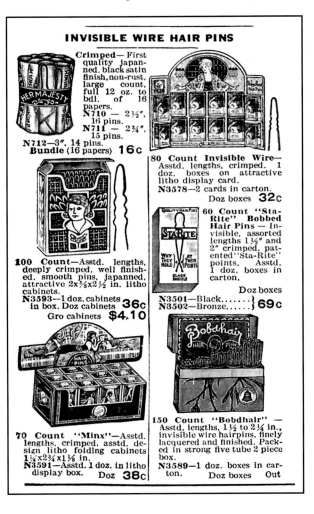

INVISIBLE WIRE HAIR PINS

Crimped — First quality japanned, black satin finish, non-rust, large count, full 12 oz. to bdl. of 16 papers.
N710 — 2½", 16 pins.
N711 — 2¾", 15 pins.
N712—3", 14 pins.
Bundle (16 papers) **16c**

100 Count—Asstd. lengths, deeply crimped, well finished, smooth pins, japanned, attractive 2x⅝x2½ in. litho cabinets.
N3593—1 doz. cabinets in box. Doz cabinets **36c**
Gro cabinets **$4.10**

70 Count "Minx"—Asstd. lengths, crimped, asstd. design litho folding cabinets 1¼x2¾x1⅛ in.
N3591—Asstd. 1 doz. in litho display box. Doz **38c**

80 Count Invisible Wire— Asstd. lengths, crimped. 1 doz. boxes on attractive litho display card.
N3578—2 cards in carton. Doz boxes **32c**

60 Count "Sta-Rite" Bobbed Hair Pins — Invisible, assorted lengths 1½" and 2" crimped, patented "Sta-Rite" points. Asstd. 1 doz. boxes in carton.
Doz boxes
N3501—Black......
N3502—Bronze.....} **69c**

150 Count "Bobdhair" — Asstd. lengths, 1½ to 2¼ in., invisible wire hairpins, finely lacquered and finished. Packed in strong five tube 2 piece box.
N3589—1 doz. boxes in carton. Doz boxes Out

Manicure sets complete with a tray, powder box, different size jars that could be used for cold cream, powdered pumice, cuticle-ice, etc plus utensils for grooming the nails were a "must" in the Victorian era. Some of them even came in presentation boxes and the one shown in the photos below is an extremely rare item. The pieces are decorated in a moriage fashion and the fact that it is still in the original box adds greatly to its value.

Shaving mugs were popular utensils in the Victorian era that stretched from the 1860s to the early twentieth century. Men used straight razors that made shaving difficult and even perilous at times. In fact, many men preferred to be shaved at the local barbershop and some even kept a spare shaving mug there.

King Camp Gillette introduced the safety razor and disposable blade in 1903, and by 1906, his company was manufacturing nearly 250,000 razors and over one million blades annually. Soon after, straight razors fell into disfavor, and the shaving mug was no longer needed.

Some shaving mugs were sold separately while others could be purchased in gift sets. Items that might be found in a gift box were a brush or two, straight razor, mirror, comb, manicure scissors, razor holder, and corn knife as well as a shaving mug.

In the book *Manners Culture and Dress* from 1891, a description of a gentleman's dressing room was given: "The arrangements of a gentleman's dressing-room are similar in most respects to those of the lady's dressing-room, the difference being only in small matters. In a gentleman's toilet — razors, shaving-soap, shaving brush, and a small tin pot for hot water, also packages of paper, on which to wipe razors. Cheap razors are a failure as they soon lose their edge. It has been suggested as an excellent plan to have a case of seven razors — one for each day of the week — so that they are all equally used."

Shaving mugs have been found in several shapes with all types of decoration from scenic to floral designs. Two-piece shaving mugs were also produced but are extremely difficult to find. The

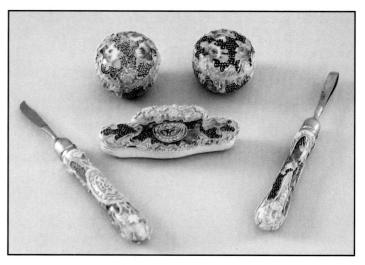

Manicure set: closed case (above left); open case (below left); close-up of items inside (above right); close-up of detail on nail buffer (below right).

An assortment of shaving mugs.

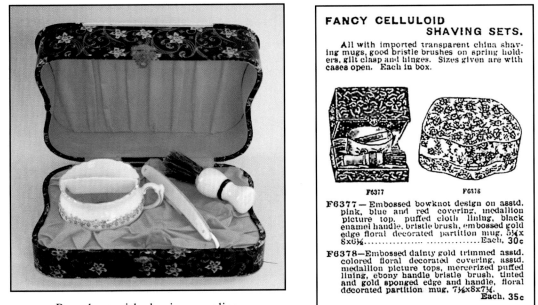

Boxed set with shaving supplies.

FANCY CELLULOID
SHAVING SETS.

All with imported transparent china shaving mugs, good bristle brushes on spring holders, gilt clasp and hinges. Sizes given are with cases open. Each in box.

F6377   F6378

F6377—Embossed bowknot design on asstd. pink, blue and red covering, medallion picture top, puffed cloth lining, black enamel handle, bristle brush, embossed gold edge floral decorated partition mug, 5¼x 8x6¼......................................Each, 30c

F6378—Embossed dainty gold trimmed asstd. colored floral decorated covering, asstd. medallion picture tops, mercerized puffed lining, ebony handle bristle brush, tinted and gold sponged edge and handle, floral decorated partition mug, 7½x8x7¼.
....Each, 35c

Two-piece shaving mug.

so-called "scuttle" mugs have separate compartments for water and soap.

During the Victorian era mustache cups were popular. Mustache cups were sold individually or with sets of dinnerware. They first became popular in the United States around 1850 and their popularity peaked around 1890.

Men's mustaches were waxed, curled, and even dyed! There were even mustache curlers and mustache spoons. The molded ledge on this special cup allowed the gentleman's mustache to rest there so that he could drink his beverage without letting his mustache touch the hot liquid.

Some of these cups have a decidedly masculine look while many are definitely feminine in appearance. Probably, the lady of the house wanted the cup to match her dinnerware at the table.

There are left-handed mustache cups but these are extremely rare to find.

Spittoons are another unusual item to find. Some people refer to them as cuspidors after the Portuguese word meaning "to spit." But the American term is usually spittoon. There was a time when one was found in most homes and public places. They were found in all sizes and in all kinds of material. Most of the Nippon marked ones are small in size and were preferred by the ladies.

There was chewing tobacco for men and snuff for ladies. Snuff was dried powdered tobacco that was inserted into the nostrils. This made expectoration a necessity, and ladies would carry a small spittoon or spit cup in their hand just for this purpose.

Potpourri jars were also popular during the period when Nippon marked items were manufactured. A potpourri jar should always have two covers to be a complete item. The top cover has pierced holes while the inner cover is solid. A potpourri mixture is placed in the jar and when the solid cover is

Two mustache cups, floral and scenic.

Ladies' spittoons.

removed the aroma of spiced dried flower petals would permeate throughout the house.

Frequent bathing was not considered necessary during this time. Actually the Saturday night bath was just coming into vogue so potpourri jars were probably a necessity!

Another confusing collectible is the open salt dish. It is sometimes mixed up with a butter pat, nut cup, or coaster, each of which is bigger in size.

Years ago, celery and relish sets came complete with matching salts. However, it is also possible that individual salts could have been purchased. The open salt dish is just about the smallest and most inexpensive piece of Nippon you can purchase today and yet salt has been a valuable product to mankind throughout the ages.

Salt comes from the word salarium which is equivalent to our word salary. Salt was used as medium of exchange years ago; in fact, ancient Roman army troops were each given a salt allotment.

Salt is dug from the earth and harvested from the sea. Over time whole seas have dried up and salt was left behind. It is used to treat sore throats, absorb wine spills, it keeps sidewalks from freezing, it seasons our food, aids in digestion, and we can't exist without it. Salt is even used in religious rites.

Open salts are diverse and can be found with many different designs decorated on them: flowers, celery stalks, radishes, birds, scenes, and even the Capitol Building in Washington, D.C. Some are found with ball feet, a few have a pedestal base. And there are those that even have reticulated (cut out) handles.

Every time we buy a piece of Nippon we're buying a piece of history. There is a limited amount available and as more and more people collect it there will be fewer and fewer pieces to be found. But with each one we do find, there is a story about its beginning and where it's been for the last 100 years. If only our Nippon could talk.

Open salt.

Potpourri jar, open and closed.

Reproductions, fakes, and fantasy pieces of Nippon are found from coast to coast. Imitations seem to be everywhere and often bear a price tag comparable to geniune Nippon pieces.

What's the difference between the three? A reproduction duplicates an exact pattern or mold, a fake has a pattern on it that never existed on an original item or is in a different shape than a real piece, and a fantasy piece is one that never existed such as an oyster plate, kerosene lamp, and wine cooler.

These items are currently manufactured in both China and Japan and, to date, more than 80 patterns have been found in a variety of pieces. The majority of the wares are of poor quality, the gold is not quite the right color, the weight is a bit heavier than the genuine pieces, and the artistic workmanship is lacking. The items just don't feel right to the experienced collector.

The manufacturers usually have the fake Nippon mark placed under the glaze and attach a paper label to indicate the country of origin. The labels are later removed and magically the item becomes a piece of "Nippon." And all of this is perfectly legal the way our current customs rules are written. If the intent is not to deceive, why would a "Nippon" backstamp be placed under the glaze?

Until recently, most of the fake marks have been knock-offs of old Noritake Company back-stamps. They all look something like the real ones but not quite identical. However, the Chinese manufacturers, and American repro wholesalers soon made it exactly like the real one. There is now a "M" in wreath mark undetectable from the genuine one. There are also patterns and molds that have definitely been copied from Nippon era ones. In fact, if you place genuine items in these patterns next to the fake ones, it can be difficult to tell which is which from a distance.

Over the years, the Noritake Company and the International Nippon Collectors Club have waged a war against these falsely marked items and have been somewhat successful. However, now these items are being manufactured without any type of Nippon backstamp, and dealers are selling them as unmarked Nippon.

A while back when all the fake marks were flooding the market, I felt that we were at least safe buying unmarked pieces if they appeared to be from the Nippon era. That's no longer the case. Unless you're an expert, I would advise you not to buy unmarked items.

Know what you are buying or know whom you are buying from. Most dealers are honest, and those who do not handle a lot of Nippon may also have purchased some of these items without knowing that they were reproduction pieces. Give them the

Left: The hexagonal cracker jar on the right is a reproduction of the genuine one shown on the left. There are some differences, such as the color of the gold trim and the fake item is heavier than the original. This piece is 7½" tall and can be purchased from the wholesaler for $15.00. Right: The reproduction has a gold "Made in China" sticker on it. The dealer can easily remove the sticker and at this point it becomes an "unmarked" piece of Nippon. The bottom of the item shows evidence of sloppy glazing.

benefit of the doubt. But if you find these items in great abundance at any one dealer's shop or booth at a show, and they are not marked as reproductions, run, don't walk from this person! If in doubt, ask for a written guarantee with return privileges.

Subscribe to antiques trade newspapers and magazines for up-to-the-minute information. Join the INCC (International Nippon Collectors Club) and ask other collectors and dealers for information. If you have a computer, check out the INCC website (www.nipponcollectorsclub.com) for these fakes. Get to know the look and feel of the fakes as compared to the genuine article.

More than fifty different fake patterns were shown in the *Collector's Encyclopedia of Nippon Porcelain, Fifth Series,* and collectors and dealers should refer to this volume for those reproductions and the fake marks found on them. Since the *Fifth Series* was published, many new fakes have appeared on the market and are included in this book. Collectors and dealers should spend time familiarizing themselves with the following photos to avoid making the costly mistakes.

This is probably the most dangerous of all the fakes to collectors. The cobalt trim is exceptional and from a distance one would not know that this was not a genuine piece of Nippon. It is so good that several seasoned collectors have already purchased it by mistake. The chocolate pot is 9" tall and although the wholesaler's catalog lists a $30.00 price for it, I managed to purchase it for $20.00!

Above: Notice the slight gold wear on the genuine cracker jar on the left. Below: This photograph shows the difference of the covers. The fake piece is on the right. Probably as soon as this book is published the manufacturer will correct this defect and make it look like the real one.

This is a close-up of the cobalt and hand-painted work on the piece. Collectors can tell that it is a fake item just by touching the piece, as it is has a rougher surface than the real items.

Left: This milk pitcher measures 7" tall and looks authentic. The wholesale cost was $15.00. Right: The same mold was used for this milk pitcher on the left. It too is 7" tall and cost $15.00.

A pair of vases. The first is 10¼" tall; the one on the right is 12" tall. Both have the same pattern. The smaller vase cost $12.50, and the larger one sold for $15.00.

This photograph shows the back of the vase shown in the photo on the left.

This vase has the same mold as the one shown on the far left and comes in both 8" and 12" sizes. They range in price from $15.00 to $25.00.

Wall pocket, 5½" tall and priced at $7.00.

Wall pocket, same mold as on left, 5½" tall, $7.00.

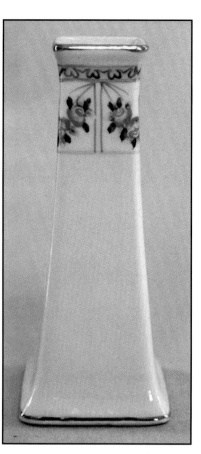

This is a small two-piece covered box and would most likely not fool most collectors, but it is marked with a green M in wreath mark.

Called a vase in the wholesaler's catalog, however most collectors would refer to this as an open hatpin holder. It is 5" tall and costs $3.50.

Stickpin holder, 2½" tall, $3.50.

Called a fish bowl in catalogs, most collectors would think it was a jardiniere. The large one is 10¼" wide x 8" tall and has a very impressive price, $25.50 wholesale. The small bowl is 2¼" tall and sells for $3.50.

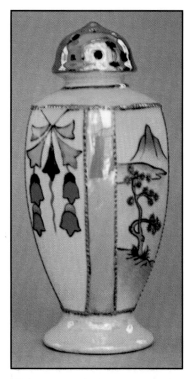

This sugar shaker has an Art Deco type decoration. It is 6" tall and wholesales for $6.25. It has the green M in wreath mark.

This 13" vase is marked with a green M in wreath mark and wholesales for $12.50.

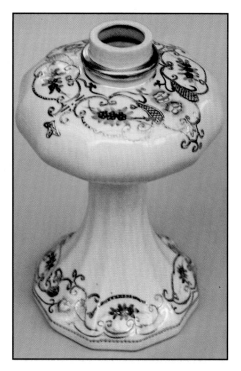

Another fantasy item is this kerosene lamp. It can be purchased as shown or as a complete lamp that is even electrified. No such item was ever manufactured during the Nippon era.

This fantasy item is called a wine cooler. It is 7" tall and costs $24.00.

This small vase is 7½" tall and costs $6.50.

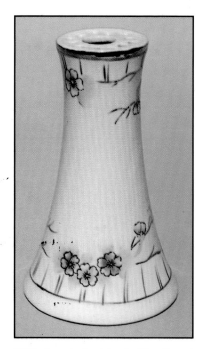

This hatpin holder is 5" tall and costs $4.50.

This two-piece covered jar is not typical of any Nippon wares and most likely will not fool collectors although it does bear the green M in wreath mark.

Wall pocket, 5" tall and priced at $7.50.

Small two-piece covered dish. This pattern is not being manufactured anymore.

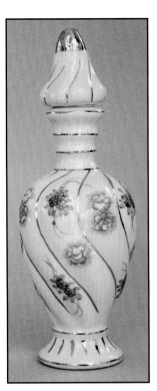

Perfume bottle, 8" tall with stopper, $7.50.

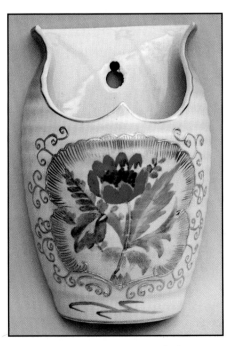

Double wall pocket, 8" tall, $11.00.

Fantasy piece, oyster dish, 9" wide, $7.00.

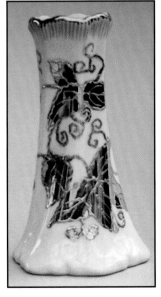

Open hatpin holder, 5" tall, $5.00.

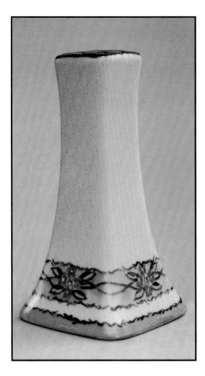

Open hatpin holder, 4¾" tall, $4.50.

This photo shows a genuine Nippon piece on the left and the fake piece on the right. Patterns are similar and very confusing for collectors.

Hatpin holder, floral and heavily beaded, 6" tall, wholesale price is $6.75.

This photo was sent to me by a collector, and although the photo is not that good, I wanted to include it to show readers that this gold-beaded wall pocket exists. The wholesaler's catalog indicates that it is 8½" tall and costs $11.00.

Tankard, 12½" tall, has hour-glass in wreath mark

The pattern shown on this huge wall pocket is found on many items. Its width is 8". This piece looks like a large vase sawed in half, and it wholesales for $9.75.

This hexagonal shaped two-piece floral tea strainer is very similar to genuine pieces.

Left: This photo shows a fantasy oyster plate that is decorated in both a scenic and floral decoration. It is intended for hanging on the wall. Right: Backside of the oyster plate.

BABY BUD NIPPON

1. Baby Bud Nippon; incised on doll.

2. Bara hand painted Nippon.

3. The Carpathia M Nippon.

4. Cherry blossom hand painted Nippon; found in blue, green, and magenta colors.

5. Cherry blossom in a circle hand painted Nippon.

6. Chikusa hand painted Nippon.

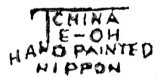

7. China E-OH hand painted Nippon; found in blue and green colors.

8. Crown (pointed), hand painted Nippon; found in green and blue colors.

9. Crown Nippon (pointed) made in Nippon; found in green and blue colors.

10. Crown (square), hand painted Nippon; found in green and green with red colors.

11. Chubby LW & Co. Nippon; found on dolls. (Louis Wolf & Co.)

NIPPON
D

12. D Nippon.

13. Dolly sticker found on Nippon's Dolly dolls; sold by Morimura Bros.

14. Double T Diamond Nippon.

15. Double T Diamond in circle Nippon.

16. Dowsie Nippon.

17. EE Nippon.

18. Elite B hand painted Nippon.

19. FY 401 Nippon; found on dolls.

20. FY 405 Nippon; found on dolls.

21. G in a circle hand painted Nippon.

22. Gloria L.W. & Co. hand painted Nippon (Louis Wolf Co., Boston, Mass. & N.Y.C.).

23. Hand painted Nippon.

24. Hand painted Nippon.

HAND PAINTED

NIPPON

25. Hand painted Nippon.

Hand Painted

NIPPON

26. Hand painted Nippon.

NIPPON

27. Hand painted Nippon.

28. Hand painted Nippon with symbol.

29. Hand painted Nippon with symbol.

30. Hand painted Nippon with symbol.

31. Hand painted Nippon with symbol.

32. Hand painted Nippon with symbol.

33. Hand painted Nippon with symbol.

34. Hand painted Nippon with symbol.

35. Hand painted Nippon with symbol.

36. Horsman No. 1 Nippon; found on dolls.

144

37. IC Nippon.

38. Imperial Nippon; found in blue and green.

39. J.M.D.S. Nippon.

40. The Jonroth Studio hand painted Nippon.

42. Kinjo Nippon.

43. Kinjo China hand painted Nippon.

41. Kid Doll M.W. & Co. Nippon.

L & CO
N I P P O N

44. L & Co Nippon.

45. L.F.H. hand painted Nippon.

L . W & Co .
N I P P O N

46. L.W. & Co. Nippon (Louis Wolf & Co., Boston, Mass & N.Y.C.).

47. M-in-wreath, hand painted Nippon (M stands for importer, Morimura Bros.); found in green, blue, magenta & gold colors. Mark used since 1911.

48. M-in-wreath hand painted Nippon, D.M. Read Co. (M stands for importer, Morimura Bros.).

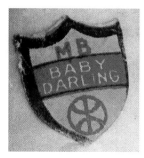

49. M B (Morimura Bros.) Baby Darling sticker; found on dolls.

MADE IN
NIPPON

51. Made in Nippon.

54. Mt. Fujiyama hand painted Nippon.

50. M. M. hand painted Nippon.

52. Maple leaf Nippon; found in green, blue, and magenta, dates back to 1891.

NIPPON

55. Nippon; found in blue, gold, and also incised into items.

53. Morimura Bros. sticker; found on Nippon items.

NIPPON
84

56. Nippon 84.

144
NIPPON

57. Nippon 144.

221
NIPPON

58. Nippon 221.

59. Nippon with symbol.

60. Nippon with symbol.

61. Nippon with symbol.

NIPPON

62. Nippon with symbol.

63. Nippon with symbol.

NO. 70018
NIPPON

64. Nippon with symbol.

65. Nippon M incised on doll (note N is written backwards); #12 denotes size of doll; M is Morimura Bros.

66. Noritake M-in-wreath Nippon; M is Morimura Bros., found in green, blue, and magenta.

67. Noritake Nippon; found in green, blue, and magenta colors.

68. Noritake Nippon; found in green, blue, and magenta colors. Mark dates from 1911, used on blank pieces (undecorated) of Nippon.

69. O.A.C. Hand painted Nippon (Okura Art China, branch of Noritake Co.).

70. Oriental china Nippon.

71. Pagoda hand painted Nippon.

PATENT
NO 30441
NIPPON

72. Patent No. 30441 Nippon.

73. Paulownia flowers and leaves hand painted Nippon (crest used by Empress of Japan, kiri no mon); found in a green/red color.

74. Paulownia flowers and leaves, hand painted Nippon (crest used by Empress of Japan, kiri no mon).

75. Pickard etched china, Noritake .Nippon.; Pickard mark is in black; Noritake/ Nippon mark is blue in color.

76. W.A. Pickard hand painted china Nippon.

77. W.A. Pickard hand painted china, Noritake Nippon; Pickard mark printed in black, Noritake Nippon in magenta.

78. Queue San Baby sticker; found on Nippon dolls.

79. RC Nippon; RC stands for Royal Crockery (fine china).

80. RC hand painted Nippon combination of both red and green colors. RC stands for Royal Crockery (fine china). Mark used since 1911.

81. RC Noritake Nippon hand painted; found in green and blue. RC stands for Royal Crockery (fine china). This mark has been in existence since 1911.

82. RC Noritake Nippon, registered in 1911. RC stands for Royal Crockery (fine china).

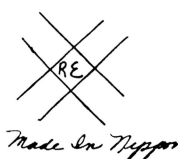

83. RE Nippon.

84. Rising Sun Nippon; mark used since 1911.

85. Royal dragon Nippon.

86. Royal dragon Nippon studio hand painted.

87. Royal Kaga Nippon.

88. Royal Kinran Nippon; found in blue, gold colors, made for domestic market in Japan since 1906.

89. Royal Kinran Crown Nippon; found in blue, gold, and green colors, made for domestic market in Japan since 1906.

90. Royal Moriye Nippon; found in green and blue colors.

91. Royal Nishiki Nippon; made for domestic market in Japan since 1906.

92. Royal Satsuma Nippon (cross within a ring, crest of House of Satsuma); made for domestic market in Japan since 1906.

93. Royal Sometuke Nippon; made for domestic market in Japan since 1906.

94. Royal Sometuke Nippon Sicily.

95. RS Nippon; found on coralene pieces.

96. S & K hand painted Nippon; found in green, blue, and magenta colors.

97. S & K hand painted Nippon; found in green, blue, and magenta colors.

149

98. Shinzo Nippon.

99. Shofu Nagoya Nippon.

100. SNB Nippon.

101. SNB Nagoya Nippon.

102. Spicer Studio Akron Ohio Nippon.

103. Spoke hand painted Nippon; mark in existence as early as 1911.

104. Studio hand painted Nippon.

105. Superior hand painted Nippon.

106. T Nippon hand painted (2 ho-o birds).

107. T hand painted Nippon.

108. T-in-wreath hand painted Nippon.

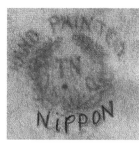

109. T N hand painted Nippon; mark is red and green.

110. T.S. hand painted Nippon.

111. TS hand painted Nippon.

112. Teacup, Made in Nippon.

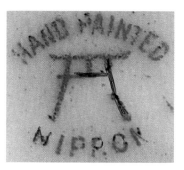

113. Torii hand painted Nippon.

114. Tree crest hand painted Nippon (Crest of Morimura family); also called Spider Mark.

115. Tree crest (also called Spider Mark) and maple leaf hand painted Nippon.

116. V Nippon, Scranton, PA.

117. The Yamato hand painted Nippon.

118. The Yamato Nippon.

119. C.G.N. hand painted Nippon; found in green.

120. F Nippon 03601 600; found incised on dolls. found in green.

121. F Nippon No. 76012 601; found incised on dolls.

122. F Nippon No. 76018 30/3; found incised on dolls.

123. FY Nippon No. 76018 403.

124. FY Nippon; found incised on dolls.

125. FY Nippon 301; found incised on dolls.

126. FY Nippon 402; found incised on dolls.

127. FY 9 Nippon 402; found incised on dolls.

128. FY Nippon 404; found incised on dolls.

129. FY Nippon 406; found incised on dolls.

130. FY Nippon 464; found incised on dolls.

131. FY Nippon No. 17604 604; found incised on dolls.

132. FY Nippon No. 70018 004; found incised on dolls.

133. FY Nippon (variation of mark) No. 70018 403; found incised on dolls.

134. FY Nippon No. 70018 406; found incised on dolls.

135. FY Nippon (variation of mark) No. 70018 406; found incised on dolls.

NO 76018
NIPPON

136. FY Nippon No. 76018; found incised on dolls, found in green.

137. Jollikid Nippon sticker (red and white), found on girl dolls; blue and white sticker found on boy dolls.

138. Ladykin Nippon sticker (red & gold); found on dolls.

NIPPON

139. Nippon (notice reversal of first N); found incised on items.

NIPPON
D13495

140. Nippon D13495; found in green.

NIPPON
E

141. Nippon E; found incised on dolls.

NIPPON
0

142. Nippon O; found incised on dolls.

5
NIPPON

143. Nippon 5; found incised on dolls.

97
NIPPON

144. Nippon 97; found incised on dolls.

98
NIPPON

145. Nippon 98; found incised on dolls.

99
NIPPON

146. Nippon 99; found incised on dolls.

101
NIPPON

147. Nippon 101; found incised on dolls.

102
NIPPON

148. Nippon 102; found incised on dolls.

105
NIPPON

149. Nippon 105; found incised on dolls.

123
NIPPON

150. Nippon 123; found incised on dolls.

144
NIPPON

151. Nippon 144 with symbol; found incised on dolls.

NIPPON

152. RE Nippon.

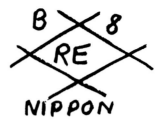

153. RE made in Nippon; found incised on dolls.

154. RE Nippon A9; found incised on dolls.

155. RE Nippon B8; found incised on dolls.

156. RE Nippon O 2; found incised on dolls.

157. Royal Hinode Nippon; found in blue.

158. Sonny sticker (gold, red, white, and blue); found on dolls.

159. Maruta Royal Blue Nippon.

160. Hand Painted Coronation Ware Nippon.

161. ATA Imperial Nippon.

162. Baby Doll, M.W. & Co. Nippon sticker; found on dolls.

163. BE, 4 Nippon.

164. Cherry blossom Nippon, similar to No. 4.

165. Cherry blossom (double) Nippon.

166. Louis Wolf & Co. Nippon.

167. C.O.N. Hand Painted Nippon.

168. FY Nippon 405; found on dolls.

169. FY Nippon 505; found on dolls.

170. FY Nippon 601; found on dolls.

171. FY Nippon 602; found on dolls.

172. FY Nippon 1602; found on dolls.

173. FY Nippon 603 NO. 76018; found on dolls.

174. Happifat Nippon sticker; found on dolls.

175. H in circle Nippon.

176. Horsman Nippon, B9; found on dolls.

177. James Studio China logo; used in conjunction with Crown Nippon mark.

178. JPL Hand Painted Nippon.

181. Komaru symbol, Hand Painted Nippon No. 16034. Note: Japanese characters are fictitious.

179. Kenilworth Studios Nippon.

180. Komaru symbol, Hand Painted Nippon; since 1912.

182. M Nippon 10; found on dolls.

183. M Nippon F24.

184. Manikin Nippon sticker; found on dolls.

185. Meiyo China Y-in-circle Nippon.

186. Nippon 3; found on dolls.

187. Nippon A3.

188. Nippon 144.

189. Nippon with symbol.

190. Nippon with symbol.

191. Nippon with symbol.

192. Nippon with symbol.

193. Nippon with symbol.

194. Nippon with symbol.

195. Nippon with symbol.

196. Nippon with symbol.

197. Hand painted Nippon with symbol.

198. Nippon with symbol, H in diamond, 14 B, P. 4.

199. Noritake M-in-wreath Nippon; M is Morimura Bros.; found in green, blue, and magenta; Derby indicates pattern.

200. Noritake M-in-wreath Nippon; M is Morimura Bros.; Sahara indicates pattern.

201. Noritake M-in-wreath Nippon; M is Morimura Bros.; The Kiva indicates pattern.

202. Noritake M-in-wreath Nippon; M is Morimura Bros.; The Metz indicates pattern.

203. Noritake M-in-wreath Nippon; M is Morimura Bros. Registered in Japan in 1912.

204. Noritake M-in-wreath Hand Painted Nippon; M is Morimura Bros.; Marguerite indicates pattern.

SEDAN

205. Noritake M-in-wreath Hand Painted Nippon; M is Morimura Bros.; Sedan indicates pattern. First dinner set made in Noritake factory 1914.

THE VITRY

206. Noritake M-in-wreath Hand Painted Nippon; M is Morimura Bros.; The Vitry indicates pattern.

207. NPMC Nippon Hand Painted.

WAVERLY

208. RC Noritake Nippon; Waverly indicates pattern.

209. RE Nippon 1120; found on dolls.

210. RE Nippon 04; found on dolls

211. RE Nippon B 9; found on dolls.

212. RE Made in Nippon A4; found on dolls.

213. RE Made in Nippon A5; found on dolls.

214. RE Made in Nippon B9; found on dolls.

215. RE Made in Nippon B1001; found on dolls.

216. Royal Kuyu Nippon.

217. S in circle Nippon.

218. Sendai Hand Painted Nippon.

219. Stouffer Hand Painted Nippon.

220. Tanega Hand Painted Nippon.

221. Torii Nippon; similar to No. 113.

222. Nagoya N & Co. Nippon.

223. Old Blue Nippon Hand Painted.

* These marks were used during the Nippon era but may have also been used after 1921.

224.* RC Noritake mark, used for domestic market in Japan by Noritake Co. since 1908. The RC stands for Royal Crockery (fine china). The symbol design is called Yajirobe (toy of balance). It symbolizes the balance in management.

225.* RC Noritake mark, used for domestic market in Japan by Noritake Co. since 1912. The RC stands for Royal Crockery (fine china). The symbol design is called Yajirobe (toy of balance). It symbolizes the balance in management.

226.* RC Nippontoki-Nagoya mark, for export since 1911. The RC stands for Royal Crockery (fine china).

227.* Made in Japan mark, used by Noritake Co., registered in London in 1908.

228.* Noritaké, made in Japan, for export to England, registered in 1908 by Noritake Co.

Noritaké

229.* Noritaké, registered in London in 1908 by Noritake Co.

230.* Noritake, made in Japan mark, registered in London in 1908.

231.* RC Japan; Noritake Co. started using the mark in 1914. It was used on items sent to India and Southeast Asia. RC stands for Royal Crockery (fine china).

232 Coalportia Nippon.

233. FY Nippon 302; found incised on dolls.

234. FY Nippon 303; found incised on dolls.

235. FY Nippon 501; found incised on dolls.

236. No. 700 Nippon HO6; found incised on dolls.

237. RE Made in Nippon C8; found incised on dolls.

238. RE Nippon, M18; found incised on dolls.

239. SK Hand Painted Made in Nippon.

240. Patent No. 17705 Royal Kinjo.

241. RS Japan; found on coralene pieces.

242. U.S. Patent 912171; found on coralene pieces.

243. U.S. Patent 912171; found on coralene pieces.

244. Kinran U.S. Patent 912171; found on coralene pieces.

245. Patent applied for No. 38257; found on coralene pieces.

246. Kinran Patent No. 16137; found on coralene pieces.

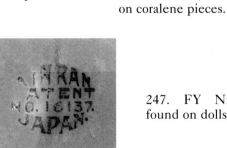

247. FY Nippon 401; found on dolls.

248. FY Nippon 409; found on dolls.

249. FY Nippon 15/4; found on dolls.

250. ESO hand-painted Nippon.

251. Miyako Nippon.

252. Royal Fuji Nippon.

253. RC Noritake, Nippon Toki Kaisha, circa 1912.

254. Komaru Nippon, circa 1906.

255. Noritake Howo, circa 1916.

256. Chikaramachi, made in Japan, circa 1912.

257. Noritake M, Japan, circa 1916.

258. Kokura, Japan, circa 1920.

259. FY Nippon No. 76018, 402; found incised on dolls.

260. FY Nippon, 11148; found incised on dolls.

261. L & Co. Nippon.

262. Yanagi Nippon, Louis Wolf & Co.

263. SK Hand Painted Nippon.

264. FY Nippon 106; found on dolls.

265. FY Nippon 203; found on dolls.

266. FY Nippon 304; found on dolls.

F. Y.
NIPPON
1604

267. FY Nippon 1604;
found on dolls.

NO 76018
NIPPON
30/3

268. Scrolled FY NO
76018 Nippon 30/3;
found on dolls.

NO 76018
NIPPON
30/6

269. Scrolled FY NO
76018 Nippon 30/6;
found on dolls.

NO 76018
NIPPON
30/8

270. Scrolled FY NO
76018 Nippon 30/8;
found on dolls.

NO 76018
NIPPON
20/0

271. Scrolled FY NO
76018 Nippon 20/0;
found on dolls.

NO 76018
103
NIPPON

272. Scrolled FY NO
76018 103 Nippon;
found on dolls.

NO 70018
NIPPON
301

273. Scrolled FY NO
70018 Nippon 301;
found on dolls.

NO 76018
NIPPON
405

274. Scrolled FY NO
76018 Nippon 405;
found on dolls.

NO 76018
NIPPON
502

275. Scrolled FY NO
76018 Nippon 502;
found on dolls.

NO 76018
NIPPON
601

276. Scrolled FY NO
76018 Nippon 601;
found on dolls.

NO 76018
NIPPON
603

277. Scrolled FY NO
76018 Nippon 603;
found on dolls.

NO 76018
NIPPON
902

278. Scrolled FY NO
76018 Nippon 902;
found on dolls.

NO 76018
NIPPON
2001

279. Scrolled FY NO
76016 Nippon 2001;
found on dolls.

BE
NIPPON

280. BE in diamond,
Nippon; found on
dolls.

A 1
RE
NIPPON

281. RE Nippon A1;
found on dolls.

O 2
RE
NIPPON

282. RE Nippon O2;
found on dolls.

283. RE Made in Nippon A10; found on dolls.

284. RE Nippon M20; found on dolls.

285. BE Nippon B10; found on dolls.

286. Horsman Nippon NO 1; found on dolls.

287. Horsman Nippon B.6; found on dolls.

288. Horsman Nippon NO-11; found on dolls.

289. JW Nippon 603; found on dolls.

290. H in diamond, Nippon 14B P.4.; found on dolls.

291. HS in an oval, Nippon 12A; found on dolls.

292. HS in an oval, Nippon 14C; found on dolls.

293. M in blossom Nippon 18; found on dolls.

294. M in blossom Nippon; found on dolls.

295. KKS in star, Nippon 3003 P.47; found on dolls.

296. KKS in star, Nippon 4003 P.53; found on dolls.

297. M in blossom, Nippon 4; found on dolls.

298. M in blossom, Nippon E20; found on dolls.

299. M Nippon 12; found on dolls.

300. M in circle, Nippon E24; found on dolls.

301. M in circle, Nippon W10; found on dolls.

**PATENT
NO. 30441
NIPPON**

302. Patent No. 30441 Nippon; found incised on dolls.

**H
NIPPON**

303. H Nippon; found incised on dolls.

**2
NIPPON**

304. 2 Nippon; found incised on dolls.

**3
NIPPON**

305. 3 Nippon; found incised on dolls.

**NIPPON
20**

306. Nippon 20; found incised on dolls.

**NIPPON
21**

307. Nippon 21; found incised on dolls.

**NIPPON
22**

308. Nippon 22; found incised on dolls.

**NIPPON
23**

309. Nippon 23; found incised on dolls.

**NIPPON
24**

310. Nippon 24; found incised on dolls.

**NO. 32
NIPPON**

311. NO. 32 Nippon; found incised on dolls.

**NIPPON
50**

312. Nippon 50; found incised on dolls.

**NIPPON
77**

313. Nippon 77; found incised on dolls.

**NIPPON
80**

314. Nippon 80; found incised on dolls.

**NIPPON
81**

315. Nippon 81; found incised on dolls.

**NIPPON
82**

316. Nippon 82; found incised on dolls.

**NIPPON
86**

317. Nippon 86; found incised on dolls.

**NIPPON
88**

318. Nippon 88; found incised on dolls.

**NIPPON
89**

319. Nippon 89; found incised on dolls.

**A 3
NIPPON**

320. A 3 Nippon; found incised on dolls.

**A 13
NIPPON**

321. A 13 Nippon; found incised on dolls.

**NIPPON
B1**

322. Nippon B1; found incised on dolls.

**NIPPON
B5**

323. Nippon B5; found incised on dolls.

**NIPPON
B10**

324. Nippon B10; found incised on dolls.

**NIPPON
B11**

325. Nippon B11; found incised on dolls.

**C 02
NIPPON**

326. C 02 Nippon; found incised on dolls.

X
NIPPON

327. X Nippon; found incised on dolls.

PATENT
NIPPON

328. Patent Nippon; found incised on dolls.

NIPPON
D

329. Nippon D; found incised on dolls.

NIPPON
87

330. Nippon 87; found incised on dolls.

93
NIPPON

331. 93 Nippon; found incised on dolls.

NIPPON
96

332. Nippon 96; found incised on dolls.

103
NIPPON

333. 103 Nippon; found incised on dolls.

NIPPON
113

334. Nippon 113; found incised on dolls.

NIPPON
122

335. Nippon 122; found incised on dolls.

222
NIPPON

336. 222 Nippon; found incised on dolls.

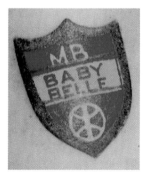

337. Sticker found on Crinoline ballerina doll.

338. Sticker found on Pixie doll.

339. Sticker found on Sweetie doll; Louis Wolf & Co.

340. Sticker found on Baby Belle doll; Morimura Bros.

341. Sticker found on Cutie doll; Louis Wolf & Co.

342. Sticker found on Kewpie doll.

343. Sticker found on the feet of Nippon Kewpie doll.

Nippon Porcelain

COBALT

Plate 3791. Pair of scenic, covered urns, each is 8¾" tall, blue mark #52, $1,500.00 – 1,800.00 each.

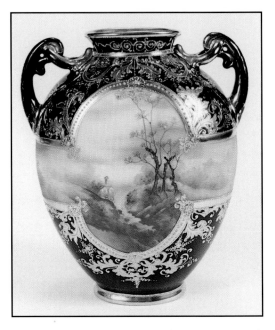

Plate 3792. Scenic vase, 10¼" tall, blue mark #52, $1,500.00 – 1,800.00.

Plate 3793. Scenic vase, 14" tall, green mark #47, $1,500.00 – 2,000.00.

Plate 3794. Scenic, bolted urn, 8½" tall, blue mark #52, $1,300.00 – 1,500.00.

Plate 3795. Photo shows underside of base of Plate 3794. Sticker is affixed to bottom that has the numbers 3950/1 printed on it. The backstamp is located directly on other wall of base. This may be an inventory sticker or perhaps this is a salesman's piece.

Plate 3796. Scenic vase, 8" tall, blue mark #47, $500.00 – 600.00.

Plate 3797. Scenic ewer, 6½" tall, blue mark #52, $500.00 – 600.00.

Plate 3798. Scenic vase, 11½" tall, mark #228, $800.00 – 950.00.

Plate 3799. Scenic vase, 8¾" tall, mark #108, $300.00 – 400.00.

Plate 3800. Scenic vase, 9" tall, mark has been scratched off, $600.00 – 700.00.

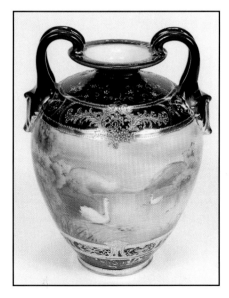

Plate 3801. Scenic vase, 9½" tall, blue mark #52, $675.00 – 800.00.

Plate 3802. Floral vase, 10" tall, green mark #52, $1,600.00 – 1,900.00.

Plate 3803. Floral vase, 5¼" tall, green mark #52, $300.00 – 400.00.

Plate 3804. Floral cracker jar, 8" tall, blue mark #52, $900.00 – 1,100.00.

Plate 3806. Floral bouillon soup cup and saucer, cup is 6" wide, unmarked, $350.00 – 450.00.

Plate 3805. Chocolate pot, 10" tall, blue mark #52, $450.00 – 550.00.

Plate 3807. Floral ferner, 10¼" wide, blue mark #52, $800.00 – 950.00.

Plate 3808. Floral bowl, 8" wide, blue mark #52, $250.00 – 350.00.

Plate 3809. Scenic ferner, 10¾" wide, green mark #47, $800.00 – 950.00.

Plate 3810. Floral dresser tray, 10¼" long, blue mark #52, $750.00 – 900.00.

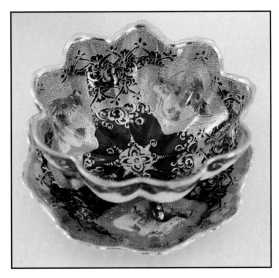

Plate 3811. Floral berry bowl and under plate, under plate is 7½" wide, blue mark #52, $600.00 – 725.00.

Plate 3812. Floral sandwich tray, 11" wide, unmarked, $350.00 – 450.00.

Plate 3813. Floral celery dish, 13¼" long, blue mark #52, $500.00 – 600.00.

Plate 3814. Floral two-piece pancake dish, bottom dish is 8¾" wide, blue mark #52, $600.00 – 750.00.

Plate 3815. Floral sandwich plate, 12" wide, green mark #52, $700.00 – 850.00.

Plate 3816. Floral plate, 10" wide, blue mark #52, $600.00 – 700.00.

Plate 3818. Silver overlay vase, 10" tall, green mark #79, $700.00 – 850.00.

Plate 3819. Scenic, silver overlay vase, 10" tall, mark #79, $750.00 – 850.00.

Plate 3817. Floral bowl, 9½" wide, blue mark #52, $600.00 – 700.00.

Plate 3820. Scenic, silver overlay humidor, 5½" tall, $900.00 – 1,100.00.

PORTRAITS

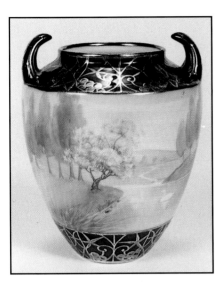

Plate 3821. Scenic, silver overlay vase, 6" tall, mark #79, $650.00 – 750.00.

Plate 3822. Left: Cobalt vase, 7½" tall, blue mark #52, $900.00 – 1,100.00. Right: Cobalt vase, 7½" tall, blue mark #52, $900.00 – 1,100.00.

Plate 3823. Cobalt vase, 6½" tall, green mark #52, $900.00 – 1,100.00.

Plate 3824. Cobalt vase, 12½" tall, blue mark #52, $1,700.00 – 1,900.00.

Plate 3825. Bolted urn, 12" tall, unmarked, $1,800.00 – 2,200.00.

Plate 3826. Bowl, 6½" wide, blue mark #52, $900.00 – 1,100.00.

Plate 3827. Vase, 5¼" tall, unmarked, $750.00 – 900.00.

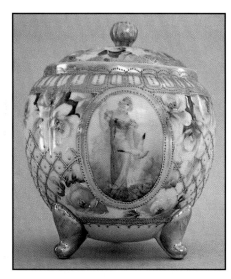

Plate 3828. Cracker jar, 7" tall, blue mark #52, $1,300.00 – 1,600.00.

Plate 3829. Vase, lady with peacock, 12¼" tall, blue mark #52, $1,800.00 – 2,200.00.

Plate 3830. Left: Wine jug (The Cardinal), 9½" tall, blue mark #52, $2,200.00 – 2,500.00. Right: Wine jug (The Cardinal), 9½" tall, blue mark #52, $2,200.00 – 2,500.00.

Plate 3831. Pair of vases (Queen Louise), 14" tall, blue mark #52, $1,600.00 – 1,800.00 each.

Plate 3832. Wall plaque, 10½" wide, blue mark #52, $900.00 – 1,100.00.

TAPESTRY

Plate 3833. Vase, 9" tall, blue mark #52, $1,400.00 – 1,600.00.

Plate 3834. Vase, 10" tall, blue mark #52, $1,100.00 – 1,300.00.

Plate 3835. Vase, 6½" tall, blue mark #52, $900.00 – 1,100.00.

Plate 3836. Vase, 5½" tall, blue mark #52, $1,400.00 – 1,600.00.

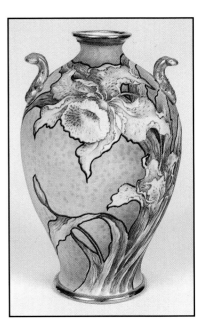

Plate 3837. Vase, 9¼" tall, blue mark #52, $2,200.00 – 2,500.00.

Plate 3838. Vase, 9¼" tall, blue mark #52, $900.00 – 1,100.00.

Plate 3839. Basket vase, 8½" tall, blue mark #52, $2,000.00 – 2,200.00.

Plate 3840. Basket vase, 8½" tall, blue mark #52, $2,200.00 – 2,400.00.

Plate 3841. Vase, 7½" tall, blue mark #52, $1,100.00 – 1,300.00.

Plate 3842. Vase, 8" tall, blue mark #52, $1,800.00 – 2,200.00.

Plate 3843. Vase, 6" tall, blue mark #52, $1,400.00 – 1,600.00.

WEDGWOOD

Plate 3845. Tea set, pot is 6" tall, green mark #47, $850.00 – 950.00.

Plate 3844. Vase, 5½" tall, blue mark #52, $1,400.00 – 1,600.00.

Plate 3846. Lavender bowl, 12¾" long, green mark #47, $850.00 – 1,000.00.

MORIAGE

Plate 3847. Floral candlestick, 6" tall, green mark #47, $250.00 – 350.00.

Plate 3848. Vase, white woodland scene, 10" tall, blue mark #47, $800.00 – 950.00.

Plate 3849. Wall plaque, white woodland scene, 9¼" wide, green mark #47, similar to Plate 3064, $900.00 – 1,050.00.

Plate 3850. Vase, white woodland scene, 5" tall, blue mark #47, $750.00 – 900.00.

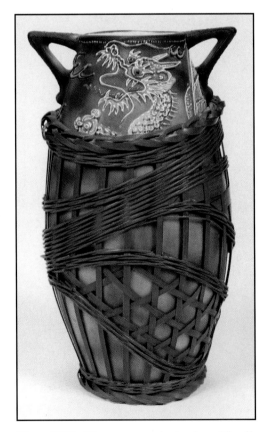

Plate 3851. Dragon vase in basket, 7" tall, mark #101, $350.00 – 400.00.

Plate 3852. Dragon dresser set, green mark #47, $900.00 – 1,100.00.

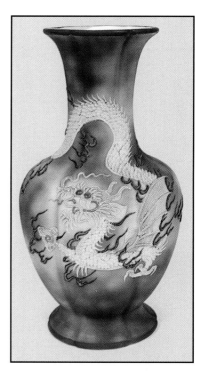

Plate 3853. Dragon vase, 10" tall, green mark #47, $550.00 – 650.00.

Plate 3854. Dragon demitasse set, five cups and saucers, green mark #47, $850.00 – 950.00.

Plate 3855. Dragon vase, 8¼" tall, green mark #47, $450.00 – 525.00.

Plate 3856. Dragon tea set, blue mark #52, $650.00 – 750.00.

Plate 3857. Vase, 10" tall, green mark #52, $1,600.00 – 1,800.00.

Plate 3858. Vase, 11½" tall, green mark #52, $1,700.00 – 2,0000.00.

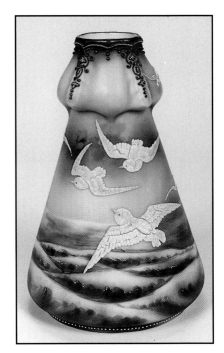

Plate 3859. Vase, 10" tall, blue mark #52, $900.00 – 1,000.00.

Plate 3860. Vase, 10" tall, green mark #52, $1,600.00 – 1,800.00.

Plate 3861. Vase, 10½" tall, unmarked, $500.00 – 600.00.

Plate 3862. Vase, 9" tall, blue mark #52, $475.00 – 575.00.

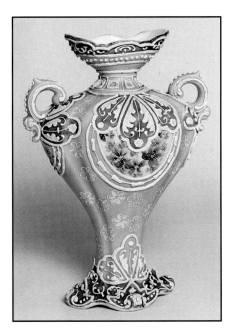

Plate 3863. Vase, 3¾" tall, unmarked, $125.00 – 160.00.

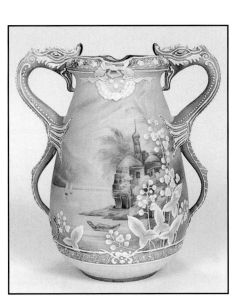

Plate 3864. Vase, 8¾" tall, blue mark #52, $1,300.00 – 1,500.00.

Plate 3865. Vase, 10½" tall, blue mark #47, $500.00 – 600.00.

Plate 3866. Vase in basket, 8¼" tall, blue mark #52, $850.00 – 950.00.

Plate 3867. Vase, 6½" tall, unmarked, $450.00 – 550.00.

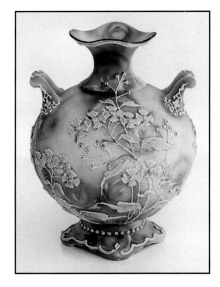

Plate 3868. Vase, 6¼" tall, blue mark #90, $450.00 – 550.00.

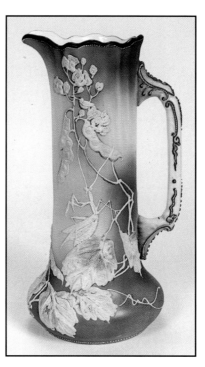

Plate 3869. Vase, 10½" tall, blue mark #52, $1,000.00 – 1,100.00.

Plate 3870. Tankard, 10½" tall, blue mark #52, $1,200.00 – 1,400.00.

Plate 3871. Vase, 7" tall, blue mark #52, $750.00 – 850.00.

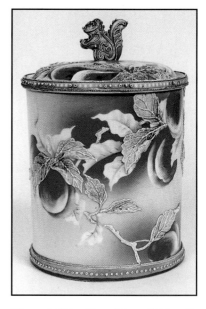

Plate 3872. Vase, 7½" tall, unmarked, $600.00 – 700.00.

Plate 3873. Humidor, 5¾" tall, blue mark #47, $1,100.00 – 1,300.00.

Plate 3874. Humidor, 7¼" tall, blue mark #52, $700.00 – 825.00.

Plate 3875. Stein, 7" tall, blue mark #52, $700.00 – 800.00.

Plate 3876. Mug, 6½" tall, unmarked, $400.00 – 500.00.

MOLDED IN RELIEF

Plate 3877. Charger, 14" wide, green mark #47, $3,400.00 – 3,600.00.

Plate 3878. Vase, 9¼" tall, blue mark #52, $950.00 – 1,050.00.

Plate 3879. Wall plaque, 10½" wide, green mark #47, $1,400.00 – 1,700.00.

Plate 3880. Wall plaque, similar to Plate 121, 10½" wide, green mark #47, $950.00 – 1,100.00.

Plate 3881. Humidor, 6½" tall, green mark #47, $1,000.00 – 1,200.00.

Left:
Plate 3882. Vase, 8¾" tall, blue mark #47, $1,000.00 – 1,200.00.

Right:
Plate 3883. Vase, 10" tall, green mark #47, $1,000.00 – 1,200.00.

Plate 3884. Vase, 6¾" tall, green mark #47, $950.00 – 1,050.00.

CORALENE

Plate 3885. Portrait wall plaque, 11" wide, mark #242, $3,000.00 – 3,500.00.

Plate 3888. Portrait wall plaque, 10¼" wide, mark #244, $3,000.00 – 3,500.00.

Plate 3889. Vase, 5½" tall, mark #245, $950.00 – 1,050.00.

Plate 3886. Portrait vase, 7" tall, mark #242, $2,000.00 – 2,400.00.

Plate 3890. Vase, 11¼" tall, mark #242, $1,100.00 – 1,300.00.

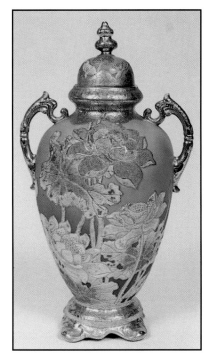

Plate 3887. Covered urn, 15" tall, mark #242, $3,000.00 – 4,000.00.

Plate 3891. Bolted ewer, 11" tall, mark #242, $1,800.00 – 2,100.00.

Plate 3892. Vase, 8¾" tall, mark #242, $1,100.00 – 1,200.00.

Plate 3893. Vase, 10" tall, mark #244, $1,300.00 – 1,500.00.

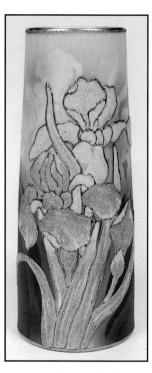

Plate 3894. Vase, 10" tall, mark #242, $1,200.00 – 1,400.00.

Plate 3895. Vase, 6¾" tall, mark #246, $650.00 – 725.00.

Plate 3896. Vase, 8" tall, mark #246, $700.00 – 900.00.

Plate 3897. Vase, 4½" tall, mark #91, $250.00 – 300.00.

Plate 3898. Vase, 10" tall, mark #244, $1,200.00 – 1,400.00.

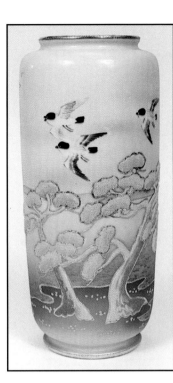

Plate 3899. Vase, 10¼" tall, mark removed, $950.00 – 1,100.00.

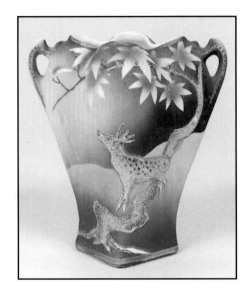

Plate 3900. Vase, 4¼" tall, mark #91, $400.00 – 500.00.

Plate 3901. Vase, 6½" tall, mark #245, $700.00 – 825.00.

Plate 3902. Vase, 6" tall, unmarked, $600.00 – 725.00.

Plate 3903. Vase, 4½" tall, mark #244, $500.00 – 625.00.

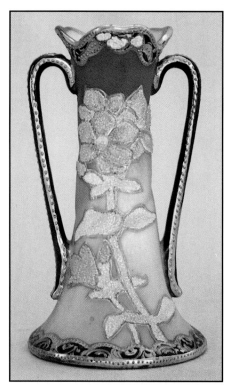

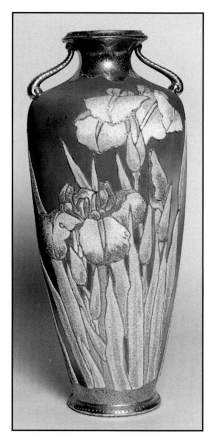

Plate 3904. Vase, 5" tall, mark #242, $500.00 – 625.00.

Plate 3905. Vase, 8¾" tall, mark #242, $900.00 – 1,050.00.

Plate 3906. Vase, 12¼" tall, mark #242, $1,300.00 – 1,500.00.

Plate 3907. Vase, 7" tall, mark #246, $575.00 – 650.00.

Plate 3908. Vase, 7" tall, mark #245, $850.00 – 950.00.

Plate 3909. Ewer, 7" tall, mark #245, $750.00 – 850.00.

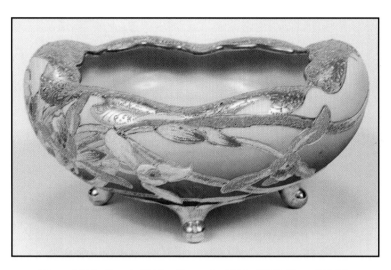

Plate 3910. Bowl, 3½" tall, mark #245, $750.00 – 850.00.

Plate 3911. Coralene wall plaque, 7" wide, mark #242, $650.00 – 750.00.

Plate 3912. Vase, 4½" tall, mark #243, $625.00 – 725.00.

FIGURAL

Plate 3913. Bird ashtray, green mark #47, $1,100.00 – 1,300.00.

Plate 3914. Two-piece candle lamp, Japanese chin dog sitting atop a suitcase, 8" tall, mark #228, $3,500.00 – 3,800.00.

Plate 3915. Bird, 4" tall, black mark #55, $300.00 – 400.00.

Plate 3916. Another view of lamp shown in Plate 3914.

SOUVENIRS

Plate 3917. Moriage vase, Del. Water Gap, Pa., 5¼" tall, green mark #47, $250.00 – 300.00.

Plate 3918. Close-up of back of vase.

Plate 3919. Celery set, Capitol at Washington, 12¾" long, green mark #47, $85.00 – 135.00.

Plate 3920. Toothpick holder, Newport, RI, 2¼" tall, green mark #47, $100.00 – 140.00.

Plate 3921. Plate, Mt. Rainier and Lake Washington, 8½" wide, mark #100, $200.00 – 300.00.

SPECIAL SCENES

Plate 3922. Humidor, Chief Joseph, 6" tall, blue mark #47, $1,200.00 – 1,400.00.

Plate 3923. Indian in canoe humidor, 7" tall, green mark #47, $1,200.00 – 1,400.00.

Plate 3924. Indian in canoe vase, 7" tall, green mark #47, $600.00 – 725.00.

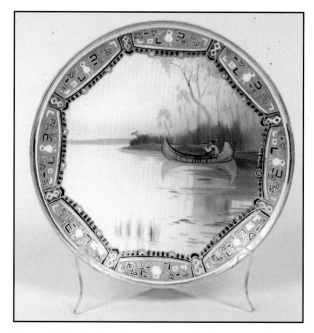

Plate 3925. Indian in canoe wall plaque, 10" wide, green mark #47, $475.00 – 575.00.

Plate 3926. Molded in relief Egyptian styled candlesticks, 8¾" tall, green mark #47, $1,500.00 – 2,000.00 each.

Plate 3927. Whiskey jug, Egyptian decoration, 6¼" tall, green mark #47, $750.00 – 900.00.

Plate 3928. Bowl, Egyptian decoration, 7¾" wide, green mark #47, $300.00 – 400.00.

Plate 3929. Vase, Egyptian decoration, 8" tall, green mark #47, $425.00 – 525.00.

Plate 3930. Smoke set, seven pieces, airplane décor, green mark #47, $1,300.00 – 1,500.00.

Plate 3931. Vase, 5½" tall, arrival of the coach scene, green mark #47, $650.00 – 750.00.

Plate 3932. Vase, 7½" tall, arrival of the coach scene, green mark #47, $650.00 – 750.00.

Plate 3933. Covered urn, woodland scene, 10½" tall, blue mark #47, $1,800.00 – 2,200.00.

Plate 3934. Humidor, woodland scene, 6¼" tall, blue mark #52, $1,400.00 – 1,600.00.

Plate 3935. Syrup, woodland scene, 4½" tall, green mark #47, $350.00 – 400.00.

Plate 3936. Vase, woodland scene, 6½" tall, green mark #47, $550.00 – 650.00.

Plate 3937. Heavily beaded vase, 4" tall, mark #70, $300.00 – 400.00.

Plate 3938. Heavily beaded creamer and sugar bowl, sugar bowl is 5½" tall, mark #89, $350.00 – 450.00.

Plate 3939. Heavily beaded vase, 9" tall, blue mark #52, $700.00 – 900.00.

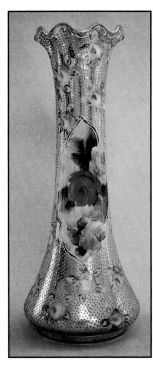

Plate 3940. Heavily beaded vase, 11" tall, mark removed, $700.00 – 900.00.

Plate 3941. Heavily beaded vase, 15" tall, blue mark #52, $850.00 – 1,000.00.

Plate 3942. Heavily beaded vase, 6" tall, green mark #52, $400.00 – 500.00.

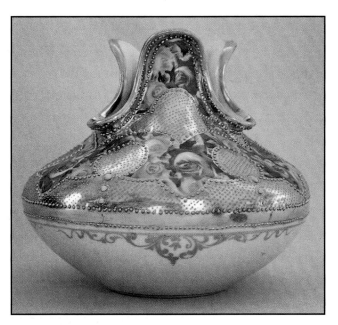

Plate 3943. Heavily beaded basket vase, 6" tall, unmarked, $400.00 – 500.00.

Plate 3944. Heavily beaded basket vase, 6" tall, unmarked, $400.00 – 500.00.

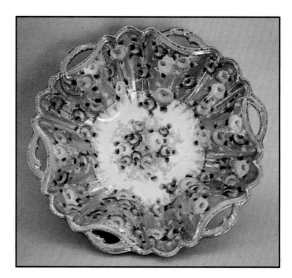

Plate 3945. Heavily beaded bowl, 10" wide, note attached says "Dad to Grandpa and Grandma 1908," mark #89, $400.00 – 500.00.

Plate 3946. Wine jug, Galle pattern, 11" tall, blue mark #52, $1,100.00 – 1,300.00.

Plate 3947. Vase, Galle pattern, 13" tall, blue mark #52, $900.00 – 1,100.00.

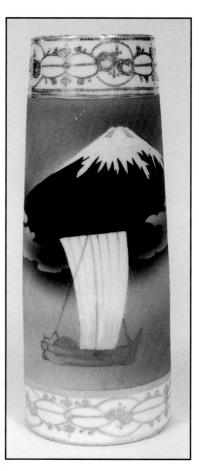

Plate 3948. Vase, Royal Kinjo, 10" tall, mark #240, $450.00 – 550.00.

URNS AND VASES

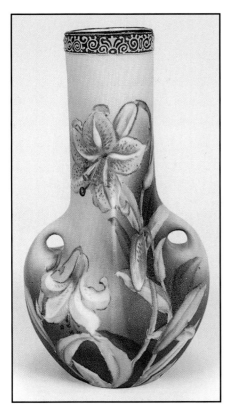

Plate 3949. Vase, Royal Kinjo, 10" tall, mark #240, $500.00 – 650.00.

Plate 3950. Pair of bolted urns, 17½" tall, green mark #47, $2,200.00 – 2,400.00 each.

Plate 3951. Bolted urn, 9" tall, gold mark #47, $500.00 – 600.00.

Plate 3952. Bolted urn, 14" tall, green mark #47, $1,400.00 – 1,600.00.

Plate 3953. Bolted covered urn, 24" tall, blue mark #52, $8,000.00 – 9,500.00.

Plate 3954. Bolted urn, 14" tall, mark is unknown, as it is not found on base, $1,500.00 – 2,000.00.

Plate 3955. Bolted urn, 28" tall, green mark #47, $10,000.00 – 12,000.00.

Plate 3956. Bolted urn, 21" tall, blue mark #52, $2,800.00 – 3,100.00.

Plate 3957. Bolted ewer, 14" tall, green mark #47, $1,500.00 – 2,000.00.

Plate 3958. Bolted covered urn, 17½" tall, blue mark #52, $2,400.00 – 2,800.00.

Plate 3959. Vase, 7½" tall, blue mark #52, $300.00 – 375.00.

Plate 3960. Vase, 9", unmarked, $400.00 – 475.00.

Plate 3961. Vase, 24" tall, blue mark #52, $4,500.00 – 5,500.00.

Plate 3962. Back of vase shown in #3961.

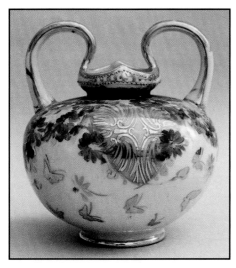

Plate 3963 Vase, 5" tall, green mark #52, $250.00 – 325.00.

Plate 3965. Pair of vases, 11" tall, blue mark #52, $600.00 – 700.00. each. Matching bolted urn, 11¾" tall, mark #70, $1,000.00 – 1,200.00.

Plate 3964. Vase, 8½" tall, mark #47, $400.00 – 500.00.

Plate 3966. Vase, 25" tall, blue mark #52, $4,500.00 – 5,500.00.

Plate 3967. Vase, 10¾" tall, blue mark #52, $400.00 – 500.00.

Plate 3968. Vase, 6" tall, blue mark #47, $250.00 – 350.00.

Plate 3969. Vase, 8½" tall, green mark #47, $300.00 – 375.00. Vase, 8" tall, green mark #47, $300.00 – 375.00.

Plate 3970. Vase, 13" tall, green mark #47, $350.00 – 425.00.

Plate 3971. Pair of vases, 6½" tall, green mark #47, $325.00 – 400.00 each.

Plate 3972. Vase, 9½" tall, blue mark #52, $350.00 – 425.00.

Plate 3973. Vase, 9" tall, blue mark #52, $350.00 – 425.00.

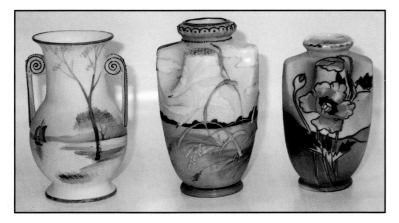

Plate 3974. Left to right: vase, 4¾" tall, green mark #47, $125.00 – 160.00; vase 5" tall, green mark #47, $150.00 – 200.00; vase, 4½" tall, green mark #47, $125.00 –160.00.

Plate 3975. Vase, 8¾" tall, green mark #47, $225.00 – 275.00.

Plate 3976. Vase, Rookwood imitation, 12" tall, green mark #52, $600.00 – 725.00.

Plate 3977. Vase, 8" tall, green mark #47, $350.00 – 450.00.

Plate 3978. Vase, 9" tall, green mark #47, $300.00 – 400.00.

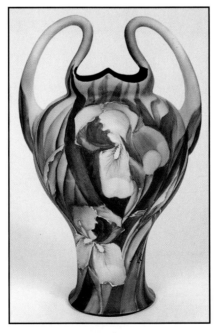

Plate 3979. Vase, Rookwood imitation, 8¾" tall, mark #88, $550.00 – 650.00.

Plate 3980. Vase, Rookwood imitation, 9½" tall, mark #88, $500.00 – 600.00.

Plate 3981. Vase, 12½" tall, blue mark #52, $800.00 –950.00.

Plate 3982. Vase, 11½" tall, green mark #47, $375.00 – 475.00.

Plate 3983. Vase, 9½" tall, blue mark #52, $475.00 – 525.00.

Plate 3984. Vase, 9½" tall, green mark #47, $475.00 – 525.00.

Plate 3985. Vase, 5½" tall, green mark #47, $125.00 – 160.00.

Plate 3986. Vase, 11" tall, green mark #47, $600.00 – 700.00.

Plate 3987. Vase, 7" tall, mark #47, $250.00 – 325.00.

Plate 3988. Vase, 8" tall, blue mark #52, $300.00 – 375.00.

Plate 3989. Vase, 10" tall, green mark #52, $425.00 – 500.00.

Plate 3990. Vase, 6½" tall, blue mark #52, $275.00 – 350.00.

Plate 3991. Vase, 7¾" tall, green mark #47, $300.00 – 375.00.

Plate 3992. Vase, 12½" tall, blue mark #52, $350.00 – 425.00.

Plate 3993. Vase, 10½" tall, unmarked, $350.00 – 425.00.

Plate 3994. Vase, 10" tall, blue mark #52, $425.00 – 500.00.

Plate 3995. Vase, 12" tall, green mark #52, $900.00 – 1,000.00.

Plate 3996. Vase, 9" tall, unmarked, $350.00 – 425.00.

Plate 3997. Vase, 9" tall, blue mark #66, $275.00 – 350.00.

Plate 3998. Vase, 11" tall, green mark #47, $400.00 – 500.00.

Plate 3999. Vase, 8¾" tall, blue mark #47, $400.00 – 500.00.

Plate 4000. Vase, 11½" tall, green mark #47, $700.00 – 850.00.

Plate 4001. Vase, 7¾" tall, blue mark #52, $550.00 – 650.00.

Plate 4002. Vase, 10" tall, green mark #47, $525.00 – 600.00.

Plate 4003. Vase, 10" tall, blue mark #52, $600.00 – 750.00.

Plate 4004. Vase, 12" tall, magenta #110, $300.00 – 400.00.

Plate 4005. Vase, 12" tall, green mark #47, $800.00 – 900.00.

Plate 4006. Vase, 5½" tall, green mark #47, $275.00 – 350.00.

Plate 4007. Vase, 7" tall, green mark #47, $325.00 – 400.00.

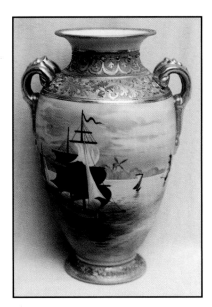

Plate 4008. Vase, 10" tall, blue mark #230, $600.00 – 725.00.

Plate 4009. Vase, 7" tall, green mark #47, $600.00 – 700.00.

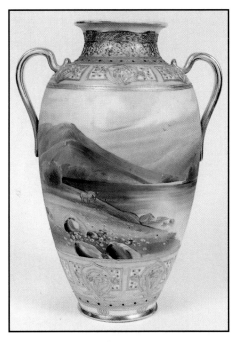

Plate 4010. Vase, 15" tall, green mark #47, $1,200.00 – 1,500.00.

Plate 4011. Vase, 15½" tall, green mark #47, $1,600.00 – 2,000.00.

Plate 4012. Vase, 6½" tall, blue mark #38, $200.00 – 260.00.

Plate 4013. Left: Vase, 5" tall, blue mark #52, $110.00 – 160.00. Right: Vase, 5" tall, blue mark #52, $110.00 –160.00.

Plate 4014. Vase, enameled trees, 7½" tall, $650.00 – 750.00.

Plate 4015. Vase, 12¼" tall, mark #52, $700.00 – 850.00.

Plate 4016. Vase, 9½" tall, green mark #47, $235.00 – 300.00.

Plate 4017. Vase, 9½" tall, green mark #47, $275.00 – 350.00.

Plate 4018. Vase, 18¼" tall, green mark #47, $1,600.00 – 1,900.00.

Plate 4019. Vase, 8¾" tall, green mark #47, $425.00 – 500.00.

Plate 4020. Vase, 6¾" tall, green mark #47, $250.00 – 325.00.

Plate 4021. Vase, 7¼" tall, mark #47, $500.00 – 625.00.

Plate 4022. Vase, 4½" tall, green mark #47, $550.00 – 700.00.

Plate 4023. Vase, 5½" tall, blue mark #47, $550.00 – 700.00.

Plate 4024. Vase, 8" tall, green mark #47, $350.00 – 450.00.

Plate 4025. Vase, 6" tall, green mark #47, $500.00 – 600.00.

Plate 4026. Vase, 8¾" tall, blue mark #52, $600.00 – 700.00.

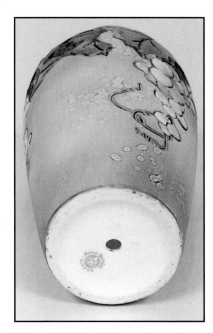

Plate 4027. Vase/factory lamp base, this photo shows drill hole of Plate 4028, mark is off to side.

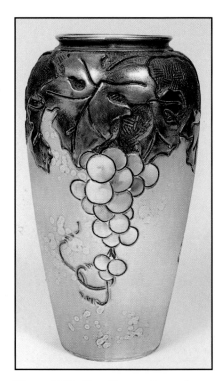

Plate 4028. Vase/factory lamp base, green mark #47, $750.00 – 850.00.

Plate 4029. Vase, 6¾" tall, blue mark #52, $550.00 – 650.00.

Plate 4030. Vase, 7½" tall, blue mark #52, $650.00 – 750.00.

Plate 4031. Vase, 8" tall, blue mark #52, $650.00 – 750.00.

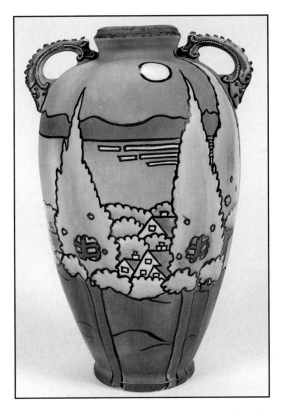

Plate 4032. Vase, 7¾" tall, blue mark #52, $675.00 – 725.00.

WALL PLAQUES

Plate 4033. Charger/wall plaque, 14" in diameter, green mark #47, signed K. Shinogi, $900.00 – 1,000.00.

Plate 4034. Wall plaque, 12" wide, green mark #47, $550.00 – 650.00.

Plate 4035. Wall plaque, 10" wide, green mark #47, $300.00 – 400.00.

Plate 4036. Wall plaque, 11" wide, green mark #47, $350.00 – 450.00.

Plate 4037. Wall plaque, 11" wide, green mark #47, $350.00 – 450.00.

Plate 4038. Wall plaque, 11" wide, green mark #47, $350.00 – 450.00.

Plate 4039. Wall plaque, 11" wide, green mark #47, $350.00 – 450.00.

Plate 4040. Wall plaque, 9" wide, green mark #47, $300.00 – 365.00.

Plate 4041. Wall plaque, 9" wide, green mark #47, $300.00 – 365.00.

Plate 4042. Wall plaque, 10" wide, green mark #47, $350.00 – 425.00.

Plate 4043. Wall plaque, 10" wide, green mark #47, $300.00 – 400.00.

Plate 4044. Wall plaque, 10" wide, green mark #47, $300.00 – 400.00.

Plate 4045. Wall plaque, 9" wide, green mark #47, $300.00 – 400.00.

Plate 4046. Wall plaque, 10" wide, green mark #47, $300.00 – 400.00.

Plate 4047. Wall plaque, 10" wide, green mark #47, $400.00 – 500.00.

Plate 4048. Wall plaque, 9" wide, blue mark #52, $300.00 – 400.00.

Plate 4049. Wall plaque, 8" wide, green mark #47, $250.00 – 325.00.

Plate 4050. Wall plaque, 9" wide, green mark #47, $275.00 – 350.00.

Plate 4051. Wall plaque, 10" wide, green mark #47, $300.00 – 400.00.

Plate 4052. Wall plaque, 10" wide, green mark #47, $300.00 – 400.00.

Plate 4053. Wall plaque, 10" wide, green mark #47, $800.00 – 900.00.

Plate 4054. Wall plaque, 8¾" wide, blue mark #47, $300.00 – 400.00.

Plate 4055. Wall plaque, 10" wide, green mark #47, $300.00 – 400.00.

Plate 4056. Wall plaque, 10" wide, green mark 347, $300.00 – 400.00.

Plate 4057. Wall plaque, 9" wide, green mark #47, $400.00 – 475.00.

Plate 4058. Wall plaque, 9½" wide, mark #109, $500.00 – 600.00.

Plate 4059. Wall plaque, 9" wide, green mark #47, $325.00 – 400.00.

Plate 4060. Wall plaque, 10" wide, green mark #47, $600.00 – 700.00.

Plate 4061. Wall plaque, 8¾" wide, green mark #47, $325.00 – 400.00.

Plate 4062. Wall plaque, 10" wide, green mark #47, $250.00 – 350.00.

Plate 4063. Wall plaque, 8¾" wide, green mark #47, $250.00 – 325.00.

Plate 4064. Wall plaque, 10" wide, green mark #47, $300.00 – 400.00.

Plate 4065. Wall plaque, 10" wide, green mark #47, $350.00 – 400.00.

Plate 4066. Wall plaque, 10" wide, green mark #47, $350.00 – 400.00.

Plate 4067. Wall plaque, 9" wide, green mark #47, $325.00 – 375.00.

Plate 4068. Wall plaque, 10" wide, green mark #47, $350.00 – 400.00.

Plate 4069. Wall plaque, 10" wide, green mark #47, $300.00 – 400.00.

Plate 4070. Wall plaque, 10" wide, green mark #47, $300.00 – 400.00.

Plate 4071. Wall plaque, 11" wide, blue mark #47, $450.00 – 550.00.

Plate 4072. Wall plaque, 10" wide, green mark #47, $300.00 – 400.00.

MISCELLANEOUS

Plate 4073. Chocolate set, six cups and saucers, green mark #52, $2,200.00 – 2,400.00.

Plate 4074. Chocolate set, six cups and saucers, blue mark #52, $1,600.00 – 1,900.00.

Plate 4075. Close-up of artist's signature found on Plate 4076.

Plate 4076. Chocolate set, six cups and saucers, blue mark #157, $1,600.00 – 1,900.00.

Plate 4077. Chocolate pot, 9¼" tall, six plate s which are 6⅜" wide, six cups and saucers, mark #38, $400.00 – 500.00.

Plate 4078. Chocolate set, pot is 8½" tall, green mark #47, $150.00 – 200.00.

Plate 4079. Chocolate set, pot is 9½" tall, set comes with six cups and saucers, Geisha girl design, mark #17, $325.00 – 425.00.

Plate 4080. Chocolate set, pot is 9" tall, set comes with six cups and saucers, green mark #47, $275.00 – 350.00.

Plate 4081. Chocolate set, five cups and saucers, pot is 9" tall, green mark #47, $275.00 – 350.00.

Plate 4082. Chocolate set, five cups and saucers, pot is 10" tall, blue mark #52, $450.00 – 550.00.

Plate 4083. Chocolate set, pot is 9" tall, six cups and saucers, blue mark #47, $700.00 – 900.00.

Plate 4084. Chocolate set, 9" tall, creamer and sugar bowl, green mark #52, $600.00 – 700.00.

Plate 4085. Chocolate set, six cups and saucers, pot is 10" tall, blue mark #52, $600.00 – 750.00.

Plate 4086. Chocolate set, comes with six cups and saucers, pot is 9¼" tall, green mark #47, $500.00 – 600.00.

Plate 4087. Tea set, pot is 5" tall, six cups and saucers, blue mark #52, $800.00 – 1,000.00.

Plate 4088. Chocolate pot, 8½" tall, magenta mark #47, $85.00 – 135.00.

Plate 4089. Tea set, six cups and saucers, mark #47, $300.00 – 400.00.

Plate 4090. Tea set, six cups, saucers and luncheon plates, pot is 7" tall, mark #111, $600.00 – 800.00.

Plate 4091. Teapot, blue mark #52, $100.00 – 140.00.

Left:
Plate 4092. Wine jug, 9½" tall, green mark #47, $900.00 – 1,100.00.

Right:
Plate 4093. Whiskey jug, 6" tall, green mark #47, $800.00 – 925.00.

Plate 4095. Wine jug, 9½" tall, green mark #47, $900.00 – 1,100.00.

Plate 4094. Wine jug, 11" tall, blue mark #47, $1,300.00 – 1,450.00.

Plate 4096. Whiskey jug, 6¾" tall, mark #47, $900.00 – 1,000.00.

Plate 4097. Pitcher, 9¼" tall, blue mark #52, $500.00 – 600.00.

Plate 4098. Pitcher, 6" blue mark #52, $550.00 – 650.00.

Plate 4099. Pitcher, 8" tall, unmarked, $375.00 – 475.00.

Plate 4100. Pitcher, 8½" tall, mark scratched off, $375.00 – 475.00.

Plate 4101. Tankard, 9¾" tall, green mark #50, $275.00 – 350.00.

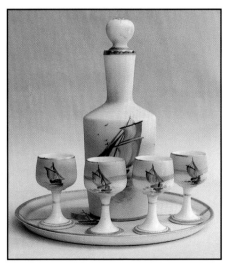

Plate 4102. Decanter set, 7¾" tall, green mark #47, $1,500.00 – 1,800.00.

Plate 4103. Carafe set, mark #47, $1,000.00 – 1,200.00.

Plate 4104. Tankard, 11½", blue mark #52, $800.00 – 950.00.

Left:
Plate 4105. Mug, 5½" tall, green mark #47, $350.00 – 450.00.

Right:
Plate 4106. Mug, 4½" tall, blue mark #52, $300.00 – 400.00.

Plate 4107. Mug, 4½" tall, green mark #52, $300.00 – 400.00.

Plate 4108. Mug, 5¾" tall, green mark #47, $350.00 – 450.00.

Plate 4109. Mug, 5½" tall, gold mark #88, $325.00 – 425.00.

Plate 4111. Dresser set, mark #228, $1,300.00 – 1,500.00.

Plate 4110. Hanging hatpin holder, 7" tall, blue mark #52, $450.00 – 575.00.

Plate 4113. Powder box, 5" wide, green mark #47, $400.00 – 500.00. Large powder box, 7" wide, green mark #47, $500.00 – 650.00.

Plate 4112. Dresser set, tray is 7" round, mark #47, $300.00 – 375.00.

Plate 4114. Dresser set, tray is 10¼" long, all items are marked blue #47 except pin dish which is green mark #47, hatpin is 4¾" tall, $950.00 – 1,100.00.

Plate 4115. Dresser set, blue mark #47, $850.00 – 950.00.

Plate 4116. Powder shaker, 4½" tall, mark 347, $300.00 – 400.00.

Plate 4117. Powder box. 3" tall, mark #52, $300.00 – 400.00.

Plate 4118. Vanity organizer, 7½" long, blue mark #52, $300.00 – 400.00.

Plate 4119. Powder box, 3¼" wide, green mark #47, $60.00 – 85.00.

Plate 4120. Dresser set, tray is 6¼" wide, blue mark #84, $120.00 – 160.00.

Plate 4121. Powder box, 5" in diameter, blue mark #52, $100.00 – 140.00.

Plate 4122. Powder box, 5" in diameter, blue mark #47, $575.00 – 675.00.

Plate 4123. Hair receiver, 4½" in diameter, green mark #47, $60.00 – 85.00.

Plate 4124. Stickpin holder, 1¾" tall, blue mark #47, $200.00 – 275.00.

Plate 4125.

Top row: Trinket box, 2" tall, has initials F.J.W. written on bottom, blue mark #84, $80.00 – 115.00. Trinket box, 2" tall, blue mark #84, $50.00 – 75.00. Trinket box, 2" tall, blue mark #84, $60.00 – 80.00. Trinket box, 2" tall, blue mark #84, $60.00 – 80.00.

Bottom row: Trinket box, 2" tall, blue mark #68, $60.00 – 80.00. Trinket box, 2" tall, blue mark #80, $60.00 – 80.00. Trinket box, 2" tall, blue mark #52, $80.00 – 115.00. Trinket box, 2" tall, green mark #47, $60.00 – 80.00.

Plate 4126.

Top row: Trinket box, 2¾" tall, green mark #47, $85.00 – 125.00. Trinket box, 2¾" tall, green mark #47, $85.00 – 125.00.

Middle row: Trinket box, 2¾" wide, blue mark #84, $85.00 –125.00. Trinket box, 2¾" wide, green mark #47, $85.00 – 125.00. Trinket box, 2¾" wide, green mark #47, $85.00 – 125.00.

Last row: Trinket box, 2½" wide, green mark #47, $80.00 – 115.00. Trinket box, 2½" wide, unmarked, $80.00 – 115.00.

Plate 4128. Chamberstick, 4" diameter, magenta mark #47, $85.00 – 135.00.

Plate 4127. Five small boxes, each is 1¼" tall, green mark #47, $60.00 – 85.00 each.

Plate 4129. Chamberstick, 6" wide, blue mark #52, $200.00 – 260.00.

Plate 4130. Pair of candlesticks, 8" tall, green mark #47, $450.00 – 550.00 a pair.

Plate 4131. Pair of candlesticks, 6½" tall, green mark #47, $300.00 – 400.00 a pair.

Plate 4132. Chamberstick, 6½" wide, blue mark #52, $135.00 – 175.00.

Plate 4133. Ferner, 5¾" tall, has lion head handles, green mark #47, $425.00 – 500.00.

Plate 4134. Ferner, 9½" handle to handle, green mark #50, $425.00 – 500.00.

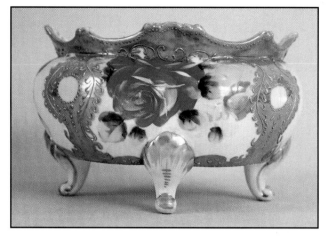

Plate 4135. Ferner, 5¾" wide, unmarked, $300.00 – 400.00.

Plate 4136. Ferner, 6¾" wide, green mark #47, $300.00 – 400.00.

Left:
Plate 4137. Humidor, 6½" tall, green mark #47, $850.00 – 950.00.

Right:
Plate 4138. Humidor, 7½" tall, blue mark #47, $850.00 – 950.00.

Left:
Plate 4139. Humidor, 5½" tall, green mark #47, $650.00 – 750.00.

Right:
Plate 4140. Humidor, 7½" tall, green mark #47, $600.00 – 700.00.

Plate 4141. Smoke set, green mark #47, $900.00 – 1,000.00.

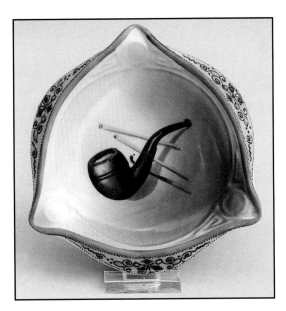

Plate 4142. Ashtray, 5¼" tall, green mark #47, $150.00 – 200.00.

Plate 4143. Ashtray, 5¼" tall, mark #17, $200.00 – 250.00.

Plate 4144. Smoke set, mark #47, $800.00 – 925.00.

Left:
Plate 4145. Hanging match box holder, 4½" long, green mark #47, $175.00 – 235.00.

Right:
Plate 4146. Cigarette box, green mark #47, $250.00 – 350.00. Ashtray, green mark #47, $250.00 – 350.00.

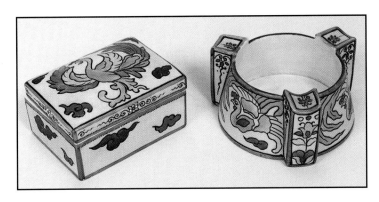

Left:
Plate 4147. Cigarette box, 5½" long, green mark #47, $550.00 – 650.00.

Right:
Plate 4148. Hanging double match box holder, mark #47, $250.00 – 325.00.

Plate 4150. Sugar bowl and creamer, sugar bowl is 6½" wide, unmarked, $150.00 – 200.00.

Plate 4149. Cigarette box, 4½" wide, mark #38, $550.00 – 650.00.

Plate 4152. Creamer, 3" tall, mark #80, $25.00 – 35.00. Creamer, 3" tall, mark #17, $25.00 – 35.00.

Plate 4151. Creamer, 5½" wide, green mark #47, $30.00 – 40.00.

Plate 4153. Sugar bowl and creamer, green mark #47, $100.00 – 150.00.

Plate 4154. Sugar bowl and creamer, green mark #47, $150.00 – 200.00.

Plate 4155. Sugar bowl, 5½" wide, green mark #47, $30.00 – 40.00.

Plate 4156. Toothpick holder, 2⅜" tall, green mark #47, $65.00 – 100.00. Toothpick holder, 2" tall, blue mark #52, $65.00 – 100.00. Toothpick holder, 2⅜" tall, green mark #47, $65.00 – 100.00.

Plate 4157. Toothpick holder, 2½" tall, blue mark #254, $65.00 – 100.00. Toothpick holder, 2½" tall, green mark #47, $65.00 – 100.00. Toothpick holder, 2¼" tall, green mark #47, $65.00 – 100.00. Toothpick holder, 2½" tall, green mark #47, $65.00 – 100.00.

Plate 4158. Toothpick holder, 2" tall, green mark #47, $65.00 – 100.00. Toothpick holder, 2½" tall, green mark #52, $65.00 – 100.00. Toothpick holder, 2" tall, green mark #47, $65.00 – 100.00.

Plate 4159. Toothpick holder, 2½" tall, green mark #47, $65.00 – 100.00.

Plate 4160. Toothpick holder, 2½" tall, green mark #47, $65.00 – 100.00. Toothpick holder, 2" tall, blue mark #84, $65.00 – 100.00. Toothpick holder, 2¼" tall, blue mark #84, $65.00 – 100.00.

Plate 4161. Potpourri jar, 5½" tall, blue mark #101, $200.00 – 275.00.

Plate 4162. This photo shows how the potpourri jar in Plate 4161 looks when it is open.

Plate 4163. Potpourri jar, 4" tall, green mark #47, $200.00 – 275.00.

Plate 4164. Potpourri jar, 6½" tall, green mark #47, $225.00 – 300.00.

Plate 4165. Shaving mug, 3¾" tall, green mark #47, $225.00 – 275.00. Shaving mug, 3¾" tall, green mark #47, $225.00 – 275.00.

Plate 4166. Bowl set, large bowl is 10" wide, six smaller bowls are 5" wide, blue mark #47, $175.00 – 225.00.

Plate 4167. Punchbowl with stand, 12" wide, mark #228, $750.00 – 900.00.

Plate 4168. Ice cream set, 10" pedestal bowl, six 6" small bowls, green mark #47, $200.00 – 275.00.

Plate 4169. Nappy, 7½" wide, mark #52, $175.00 – 235.00.

Plate 4170. Nappy, 7⅞" wide, green mark #47, $85.00 – 135.00.

Plate 4171. Ice cream set, master tray is 14" long, six individual dishes are 6¼" wide, green mark #47, $175.00 – 235.00.

Left:
Plate 4172. Bowl, 9½" wide, mark #81, $225.00 – 275.00.

Right:
Plate 4173. Basket bowl, 6" wide, mark #79, $100.00 – 160.00.

Left:
Plate 4174. Bowl, 6½" wide, green mark #47, $70.00 – 120.00.

Right:
Plate 4175. Bowl, 8" wide, green mark #47, $225.00 – 275.00.

Plate 4176. Bowl, 7¼" wide, unmarked, $150.00 – 200.00.

Plate 4177. Bowl, 8½" wide, mark #80, $125.00 – 160.00.

Plate 4178. Bowl, 11" with handles, green mark #47, $225.00 – 275.00.

Plate 4179 Bowl, 10" wide, green mark #47, $325.00 – 400.00.

Plate 4180. Bowl, 8" in diameter, green mark #47, $175.00 – 225.00.

Plate 4181. Bowl, 6½" wide, green mark #47, $145.00 – 180.00. Bowl, 7" wide, green mark #47, $145.00 – 180.00.

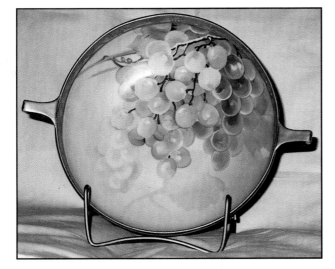

Plate 4182. Bowl, 8½" wide, green mark #47, $150.00 – 200.00.

Plate 4183. Bowl, 9½" wide, green mark #47, $150.00 – 200.00.

Plate 4184. Nut set, master bowl is 6" in diameter, individual bowls are 2¾" in diameter, blue mark #54, $175.00 – 225.00.

Plate 4185. Nappy, 4¾" wide, green mark #47, $125.00 – 160.00.

Plate 4186. Bowl, 9" wide, green mark #47, $160.00 – 220.00.

Plate 4187. Bowl, 6½" wide, green mark #47, $150.00 – 200.00.

Plate 4188. Nut set, master bowl is 6¾" wide and four individual bowls are 3" wide, mark #81, $265.00 – 325.00.

Plate 4189. Plate, 10" in diameter, blue mark #52, $375.00 – 350.00.

Plate 4190. Plate, 12" in diameter, unmarked, $400.00 – 550.00.

Plate 4191. Plate, 10" wide, blue mark #52, $325.00 – 400.00.

Plate 4192. Plate, 7¾" wide, green mark #52, $65.00 – 100.00.

Plate 4193. Plate, 12" wide, blue mark #47, $50.00 – 75.00.

Plate 4194. Plate, 6" wide, blue mark #47, $40.00 – 65.00.

Plate 4195. Cake set, comes with six individual cake plates, green mark #52, $300.00 – 375.00.

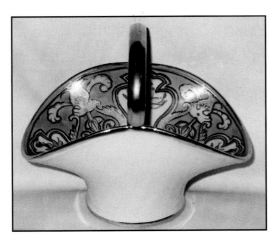

Plate 4196. Handled basket, 5½" tall, green mark #47, $85.00 – 130.00.

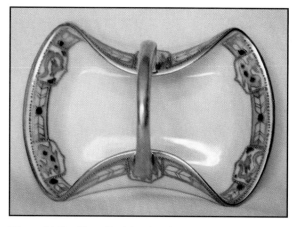

Plate 4197. Handled basket/nappy, 5" long, mark #80, $60.00 – 90.00.

Plate 4198. Cake plate, 11" wide, green mark #47, $200.00 – 275.00.

Plate 4199. Cake plate, 10" wide, green mark #47, $175.00 – 235.00.

Plate 4200. Cracker jar, 8½" wide, blue mark #52, $200.00 – 250.00.

Above: Plate 4201. Close-up of signature found on item shown in Plate 4202.

Left: Plate 4202. Platter, 16" in diameter, green mark #47, $850.00 – 1,000.00.

Plate 4203. Bon bon dish, 6½" wide, magenta mark #47, found in a marked Manning Bowman polished copper basket, #283 in old catalog, $80.00 – 120.00. Bon bon dish, 9½" wide including handles, magenta mark #47, found in a marked Manning Bowman polished copper basket, #260 in old catalog, $150.00 – 200.00.

Plate 4204. Tray, 12½" long, blue mark #52, $275.00 – 350.00.

Plate 4205. Tray, 12" in diameter, blue mark #52, $200.00 – 250.00.

Plate 4206. Condensed milk container with underplate, blue mark #52, $250.00 – 350.00.

Plate 4207. Condensed milk container with underplate, blue mark #247, $225.00 – 275.00.

Plate 4208. Jam jar, 5½" tall, green mark #47, $125.00 – 160.00.

Plate 4209. Condensed milk container with underplate, 5½" tall, green mark #47, $225.00 – 275.00. Condensed milk container with underplate, 5½" tall, green mark #47, $225.00 – 275.00.

Plate 4210. Condensed milk container with underplate, 5½" tall, green mark #47, $225.00 – 275.00.

Plate 4211. Jam jar with underplate, 5" tall, mark #47, $225.00 – 275.00.

Plate 4212. Mustard pot and underplate, 3½" tall, magenta mark #47, $50.00 – 70.00.

Plate 4213. Condiment set, tray, mustard pot, salt and pepper, tray is 6" in diameter, blue mark #84, $75.00 – 100.00.

Plate 4214. Sugar bowl, 4½" wide, $20.00 – 35.00; mustard pot, 2½" tall, $30.00 – 40.00; creamer, 2¾" wide, $20.00 – 35.00; nappy, 6½" long, $30.00 – 40.00; all have mark #84.

Plate 4215. Mustard pot with underplate, 4½" wide, mark #80, $50.00 – 70.00.

Plate 4216. Mustard pot, 4" in diameter, blue mark #52, $55.00 – 75.00.

Plate 4217. Handled basket, 7½" long, green #47, $135.00 – 175.00.

Plate 4218. Gravy boat with underplate that is 7" long, green mark #52, $150.00 – 200.00.

Plate 4219. Top row: Mayonnaise or whip cream dish with ladle, 4½" wide, blue mark #84, $65.00 – 90.00. Mayonnaise or whip cream dish with ladle, 4½" wide, magenta mark #47, $65.00 – 90.00. Bottom row: Mayonnaise or whip cream dish with ladle, 4½" wide, mark #10, $65.00 – 90.00. Mayonnaise or whip cream dish with ladle, 4½" wide, mark #84, $65.00 – 90.00.

Plate 4222. Sherbet cup and saucer, cup is 2½" tall, blue mark #52, $75.00 – 100.00.

Plate 4220. Reamer, 4¾" wide, green mark #47, $150.00 – 200.00.

Plate 4221. Reamer, 4¾" wide, green mark #47, $150.00 – 200.00.

Plate 4224. Berry bowl with underplate, plate is 8" in diameter, bowl is 7½" in diameter, mark #89, $250.00 – 300.00.

Plate 4223. Snack set (also called refreshment set, dessert set, sandwich set, toast set), blue mark #96, $400.00 – 500.00.

Plate 4225. Syrup with underplate, 4¾" tall, mark #81, $200.00 – 275.00.

Plate 4226. Toast rack, 5" long, mark #84, $150.00 – 200.00.

Plate 4227. Berry bowl with underplate, bowl is 7½" in diameter, underplate is 8" in diameter, blue mark #52, $275.00 – 350.00.

Plate 4228. Small dish, 7" wide, mark #104, $250.00 – 300.00.

Plate 4229. Tea strainer, 5½" wide, green mark #47, $150.00 – 200.00.

Left:
Plate 4230. Lamp/bolted urn, base is 14" tall, green mark #47, $900.00 – 1,100.00.

Right:
Plate 4231. Lamp, base is 14" tall, mark has been drilled out, $600.00 – 800.00.

Plate 4232. Doll, 24" tall, blue sleep eyes, mark #274, $450.00 – 500.00.

Plate 4233. Doll, 20" tall, blue sleep eyes, four teeth, mark #123, $300.00 – 350.00.

Plate 4234. Doll, 12" toddler body, painted shoes and stockings, blue sleep eyes, mark #273, $225.00 – 300.00.

Plate 4235. Doll, 15" tall, blue sleep eyes, composition body, open mouth with two upper teeth, mark #277, $300.00 – 350.00.

Plate 4236. Doll, 16" tall, blue sleep eyes, open mouth, two upper teeth, mark #287, $500.00 – 600.00.

Plate 4238. Doll, 8" tall, mark #166, $225.00 – 275.00.

Plate 4239. Doll, 9" tall, mark #55, $200.00 – 250.00.

Plate 4237. Doll, 8" tall, five piece composition body, mark #55, $140.00 – 170.00.

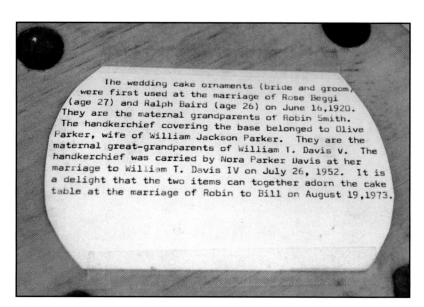

Plate 4240. Bride and groom dolls, each 5" tall, found in a dome holder with note shown in Plate 4241, mark #55, $225.00 – 275.00 a pair.

Plate 4241. Card found on base of dome holder for dolls shown in Plate 4240.

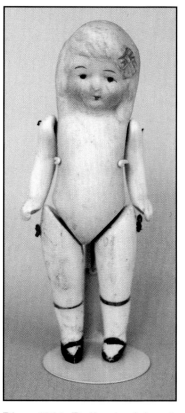

Plate 4242. Bride and groom dolls, 5¼" tall, mark #55, $225.00 – 275.00.

Plate 4243. Doll, 6¾" tall, mark #316, $130.00 – 170.00.

Plate 4244. Doll, wire jointed, 5½" tall, mark #55, $75.00 – 110.00.

Plate 4245. Doll, 5½" tall, mark #55, $120.00 – 150.00.

Plate 4246. Doll, 5" tall excluding hat, has original Baby Darling sticker, mark #55, $110.00 –125.00.

Plate 4247. Doll, 4½" tall, has original Baby Belle sticker, mark #55, $115.00 – 140.00.

Plate 4248. Doll, 4¾" tall, mark #55, $110.00 – 140.00.

Plate 4249. Doll, 6⅞" tall, mark #55, $135.00 – 165.00.

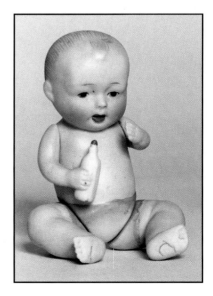

Plate 4250. Doll, 5½" tall, mark #55, $110.00 – 145.00.

Plate 4251. Child's feeding set, dish is 6½" wide, mark #84, plate, $50.00 – 70.00 and cup and saucer, $75.00 – 100.00.

Plate 4252. Child's play tea set, pot is 4" tall, mark #84, $275.00 – 300.00.

Plate 4253. Child's play chocolate set, pot is 4½" tall, mark #84, $350.00 – 400.00.

Plate 4254. Molded in relief salt and pepper set with tray, shakers are 1½" tall, child's face pattern, tray is marked #84, $150.00 – 200.00.

Plate 4255. Child's play teapot, 3" tall without handle, mark #52, $45.00 – 65.00.

Plate 4256. Child's play tea set, teapot is 3½" tall, mark #84, $300.00 – 350.00.

American Indian design: A popular collectible on Nippon porcelain; these designs include the Indian in a canoe, Indian warrior, Indian hunting wild game, and the Indian maiden.

Apricot (ume): In Japan, stands for strength and nobility, is also a symbol of good luck.

Art Deco: A style of decoration which hit its peak in Europe and America around 1925 although items were manufactured with this decor as early as 1910. The style was modernistic; geometric patterns were popular. Motifs used were shapes such as circles, rectangles, cylinders, and cones.

Art Nouveau: The name is derived from the French words, meaning "new art." During the period of 1885 – 1925, artists tended to use bolder colors, and realism was rejected. Free-flowing designs were used breaking away from the imitations of the past.

Artist signed: Items signed by the artist, most signatures appear to be those of Western artists, probably painted during the heyday of hand painting chinaware at the turn of the century.

Azalea pattern: Pattern found on Nippon items, pink azaleas with green to gray leaves and gold rims. Nippon-marked pieces match the Noritake-marked Azalea pattern items. The Azalea pattern was originally offered by the Larkin Co. to its customers as premiums.

Backstamp: Mark found on Nippon porcelain items identifying the manufacturer, exporter or importer, and country of origin.

Bamboo tree: In Japan, symbolic of strength, faithfulness, and honesty, also a good luck symbol. The bamboo resists the storm, but it yields to it and rises again.

Beading: Generally a series of clay dots applied on Nippon porcelain, very often painted over in gold. Later Nippon pieces merely had dots of enameling.

Biscuit: Clay which has been fired but not glazed.

Bisque: Same as biscuit, term also used by collectors to describe a matte finish on an item.

Blank: Greenware or bisque items devoid of decoration.

Blown-out items: This term is used by collectors and dealers for items that have a molded relief pattern embossed on by the mold in which the article was shaped. It is not actually "blown-out" as the glass items are, but the pattern is raised from the item. (See molded relief items.)

Bottger, Johann F.: A young German alchemist who supposedly discovered the value of kaolin in making porcelain. This discovery helped to revolutionize the china making industry in Europe beginning in the early 1700s.

Carp: Fish that symbolizes strength and perseverance.

Casting: The process of making reproductions by pouring slip into molds.

Cha no yu: Japanese tea ceremony.

Chargers: Archaic term for large platters or plates.

Cheese hard clay: Same as leather hard clay.

Cherry blossoms: National flower of Japan and emblem of the faithful warrior.

Ching-te-Chen: Ancient city in China where nearly a million people lived and worked with almost all devoted to the making of porcelain.

Chrysanthemum: Depicts health and longevity, the crest of the emperor of Japan. The chrysanthemum blooms late in the year and lives longer than other flowers.

Citron: Stands for wealth.

Cloisonné on porcelain: On Nippon porcelain wares it resembles the other cloisonné pieces except that it was produced on a porcelain body instead of metal. The decoration is divided into cells called cloisons. These cloisons were divided by strips of metal wire which kept the colors separated during the firing.

Cobalt oxide: Blue oxide imported to Japan after 1868 for decoration of wares. Gosu, a pebble found in Oriental riverbeds, had previously been used but was scarce and more expensive than the imported oxide. Cobalt oxide is the most powerful of all the coloring oxides for tinting.

Coralene items: Made by firing small colorless beads on the wares. Many are signed Kinran, US Patent, NBR 912171, February 9, 1909, Japan. Tiny glass beads had previously been applied to glass items in the shapes of birds, flowers, leaves, etc. and no doubt this was an attempt to copy it. Japanese coralene was patented by Alban L. Rock, an American living in Yokohama, Japan. The vitreous coating of beads gave the item a plush velvety look. The beads were permanently fired on and gave a luminescence to the design. The most popular design had been one of seaweed and coral, hence the name coralene was given to this type of design.

Crane: A symbol of good luck in Japan, also stands for marital fidelity and is an emblem of longevity.

Daffodil: A sign of spring to the Japanese.

Decalcomania: A process of transferring a wet paper print onto the surface of an item. It was made to resemble hand-painted work.

Deer: Stands for divine messenger.

Diaper pattern: Repetitive pattern of small design used on Nippon porcelain, often geometric or floral.

Dragons (ryu): A symbol of strength, goodness, and good fortune. The Japanese dragon has three claws and was thought to reside in the sky. Clouds, water, and lightning often accompany the dragon. The dragon is often portrayed in high relief using the slip trailing method of decor.

Drain mold: A mold used in making hollow ware. Liquid slip is poured into the mold until the desired thickness of the walls is achieved. The excess clay is poured out. When the item starts to shrink away from the mold, it is removed.

Drape mold: Also called flop-over mold. Used to make flat bottomed items. Moist clay is rolled out and draped over the mold. It is then pressed firmly into shape.

Dutch scenes: Popular on Nippon items, includes those of windmills, and men and women dressed in Dutch costumes.

Edo: Or Yedo, the largest city in Japan, later renamed Tokyo, meaning eastern capital.

Embossed design: See molded relief.

Enamel beading: Dots of enameling painted by the artist in gold or other colors and often made to resemble jewels, such as emeralds and rubies. Many times this raised beading will be found in brown or black colors.

Fairings: Items won or bought at fairs as souvenirs.

Feldspar: Most common rock found on earth.

Fern leaves: Symbolic of ample good fortune.

Fettles or Mold Marks: Ridges formed where sections of molds are joined at the seam. These fettles have to be removed before the item is decorated.

Finial: The top knob on a cover of an item, used to lift off the cover.

Firing: The cooking or baking of clay ware.

Flop-over mold: Same as drape mold.

Flux: An ingredient added to glaze to assist in making the item fire properly. It causes the glaze to melt at a specified temperature.

Glaze: Composed of silica, alumina, and flux, and is applied to porcelain pieces. During the firing process, the glaze joins with the clay item to form a glasslike surface. It seals the pores and makes the item impervious to liquids.

Gold trim: Has to be fired at lower temperatures or the gold would sink into the enameled decoration. If overfired, the gold becomes discolored.

Gouda ceramics: Originally made in Gouda, a province of south Holland. These items were copied on the Nippon wares and were patterned after the Art Nouveau style.

Gosu: Pebble found in Oriental riverbeds, a natural cobalt. It was used to color items until 1868 when oxidized cobalt was introduced into Japan.

Greenware: Clay which has been molded but not fired.

Hard paste porcelain: Paste meaning the body of substance, porcelain being made from clay using kaolin. This produces a hard translucent body when fired.

Ho-o bird: Sort of a bird of paradise who resides on earth and is associated with the empress of Japan. Also see Phoenix bird.

Incised backstamp: The backstamp marking is scratched into the surface of a clay item.

Incised decoration: A sharp tool or stick was used to produce the design right onto the body of the article while it was still in a state of soft clay.

Iris: The Japanese believe this flower wards off evil; associated with warriors because of its sword-like leaves.

Jasperware: See Wedgwood.

Jigger: A machine resembling a potter's wheel. Soft pliable clay is placed onto a convex revolving mold. As the wheel turns, a template is held against it, trimming off the excess clay on the outside. The revolving mold shapes the inside of the item and the template cuts the outside.

Jolley: A machine like a jigger only in reverse. The revolving mold is concave and the template forms the inside of the item. The template is lowered inside the revolving mold. The mold forms the outside surface while the template cuts the inside.

Jomon: Neolithic hunters and fishermen in Japan dating back to approximately 2500 B.C. Their pottery was hand formed and marked with an overall rope or cord pattern. It was made of unwashed clay, unglazed, and was baked in open fires.

Kaga: Province in Japan.

Kaolin: Highly refractory clay and one of the principal ingredients used in making porcelain. It is a pure white residual clay, a decomposition of granite.

Kao-ling: Chinese word meaning "the high hills," the word kaolin is derived from it.

Kiln: Oven in which pottery is fired.

Leather hard clay: Clay which is dry enough to hold its shape but still damp and moist, no longer in a plastic state, also called cheese hard.

Liquid slip: Clay in a liquid state.

Lobster: Symbol of long life.

Luster decoration: A metallic type of coloring decoration, gives an iridescent effect.

Matte finish: Also "mat" and "matt." A dull glaze having a low reflectance when fired.

McKinley Tariff Act of 1890: Chapter 1244, Section 6 states "That on and after the first day of March, eighteen hundred and ninety-one, all articles of foreign manufacture, such as are usually or ordinarily marked, stamped, branded, or labeled, and all packages containing such or other imported articles, shall, respectively, be plainly marked, stamped, branded, or labeled in legible English words, so as to indicate the country of their origin; and unless so marked, stamped, branded, or labeled, they shall not be admitted to entry."

Meiji period: Period of 1868 – 1912 in Japan when Emperor Mutsuhito reigned. It means "enlightened rule."

Middle East scenes: Designs used on Nippon pieces, featuring pyramids, deserts, palm trees, and riders on camels.

Model: The shape from which the mold is made.

Molded relief items: The pattern is embossed on the item by the mold in which the article is shaped. These items give the appearance that the pattern is caused by some type of upward pressure from the underside. Collectors often refer to these items as "blown-out."

Molds: Contain a cavity in which castings are made. They are generally made from plaster of Paris and are used for shaping clay objects. Both liquid and plastic clay may be used. The mold can also be made of clay or rubber, however, plaster was generally used as it absorbed moisture immediately from the clay. Raised ornamentation may also be formed directly in the mold.

Moriage: Refers to liquid clay (slip) relief decoration. On Nippon items this was usually done by "slip trailing" or hand rolling and shaping the clay on an item.

Morimura Brothers: Importers of Japanese wares in the United States and the sole importers of Noritake wares. It was opened in New York City in 1876 and closed in 1941.

Mutsuhito: Emperor of Japan from 1868 to 1912. His reign was called the Meiji period which meant enlightened rule.

Nagoya: A large city in Japan, location of Noritake Co.

Narcissus: Stands for good fortune.

Ningyo: Japanese name for doll, meaning human being and image.

Nippon: The name the Japanese people called their country. It comes from a Chinese phrase meaning "the source of the sun" and sounds like Neehon in Japanese.

Noritake Co.: This company produced more than 90 percent of the Nippon era wares that now exist. Their main office is located in Nagoya, Japan.

Orchid: Means hidden beauty and modesty to the Japanese.

Overglaze decoration: A design is either painted or a decal applied to an item which already has a fired glazed surface. The article is then refired to make the decoration permanent.

Pattern stamping: The design was achieved by using a special stamp or a plaster roll having the design cut into it. The design was pressed into the soft clay body of an item.

Paulownia flower: Crest of the empress of Japan.

Peach: Stands for marriage.

Peacock: Stands for elegance and beauty.

Peony: Considered the king of flowers in Japan.

Perry, Matthew, Comm., USN: Helped to fashion the Kanagawa treaty in 1854 between the United States and Japan. This treaty opened the small ports of Shimoda and Hakodate to trade. Shipwrecked sailors were also to receive good treatment and an American consul was permitted to reside at Shimoda.

Petuntse: Clay found in felspathic rocks such as granite. Its addition to porcelain made the item more durable. Petuntse is also called china stone.

Phoenix bird: Sort of bird of paradise which resides on earth and is associated with the empress of Japan. This bird appears to be a cross between a peacock, a pheasant, and a gamecock. There appear to be many designs for this bird as each artist had his own conception of how it should look. It is also a symbol to the Japanese of all that is beautiful.

Pickard Co.: A china decorating studio originally located in Chicago. This firm decorated blank wares imported from a number of countries including Nippon.

Pine tree: To the Japanese this tree is symbolic of friendship and prosperity and depicts the winter season. It is also a sign of good luck and a sign of strength.

Plastic clay: Clay in a malleable state, able to be shaped and formed without collapsing.

Plum: Stands for womanhood. Plum blossoms reflect bravery.

Porcelain: A mixture composed mainly of kaolin and petuntse which is fired at a high temperature and vitrified.

Porcelain slip: Porcelain clay in a liquid form.

Porcellaine: French adaptation of the word *porcelain*.

Porcellana: Italian word meaning cowry shell. The Chinese ware which was brought back to Venice in the fifteenth century was thought to resemble the cowry shell and was called porcellana.

Portrait items: Items decorated with portraits, many of European beauties. Some appear to be hand painted, most are decal work.

Potter's wheel: Rotating device onto which a ball of plastic clay is placed. The wheel is turned and the potter molds the clay with his hands and is capable of producing cylindrical objects.

Pottery: In its broadest sense, includes all forms of wares made from clay.

Press mold: Used to make handles, finials, figurines, etc. A two-piece mold into which soft clay is placed. The two pieces are pressed together to form items.

Relief: Molded (See molded relief items).

Royal Crockery: Name of Nippon pieces marked with RC on backstamp.

Satsuma: A sea-going principality in Japan, an area where many of the old famous kilns are found, and also a type of Japanese ware. Satsuma is a cream-colored glazed pottery which is finely crackled.

Slip: Liquid clay.

Slip trailing: A process where liquid clay was applied to porcelain via tubing or a cone-shaped device made of paper with a metal tip. A form of painting but with clay instead of paint. The slip is often applied quite heavily and gives a thick, raised appearance.

Slurry: Thick slip.

Solid casting mold: Used for shallow type items such as bowls and plates. In this type of mold, the thickness of the walls is determined by the mold and every piece is formed identically. The mold shapes both the inside and the outside of the piece and the thickness of the walls can be controlled. Solid casting can be done with either liquid or plastic clay.

Sometsuke style decoration: Items decorated with an underglaze of blue and white colors.

Sprigging: The application of small molded relief decoration to the surface of porcelain by use of liquid clay as in Jasperware.

Sprig mold: A one-piece mold used in making ornaments. Clay is fitted or poured into a mold which is incised with a design. Only one side is molded and the exposed side becomes the back of the finished item.

Taisho: Name of the period reigned over by Emperor Yoshihito in Japan from 1912 to 1926. It means "great peace."

Tapestry: A type of decor used on Nippon porcelain. A cloth was dipped into liquid slip and then stretched onto the porcelain item. During the bisque firing, the material burned off and left a textured look on the porcelain piece, resembling needlepoint in many cases. The item was then painted and fired again in the usual manner.

Template: Profile of the pattern being cut.

Throwing: The art of forming a clay object on a potter's wheel.

Tiger (tora): A symbol of longevity.

Transfer print: See Decalcomania.

Translucent: Not transparent, but clear enough to allow rays of light to pass through.

Ultraviolet lamp: Lamp used to detect cracks and hidden repairs in items.

Underglaze decoration: This type of decoration is applied on bisque china (fired once), then the item is glazed and fired again.

Victorian Age design: Decor used on some Nippon pieces, gaudy and extremely bold colors used.

Vitreous: Glass like.

Vitrify: To change into a glasslike substance due to the application of heat.

Wasters: Name given to pieces ruined or marred in the kiln.

Water lilies: Represent autumn in Japan.

Wedgwood: Term used to refer to Nippon pieces which attempt to imitate Josiah Wedgwood's Jasperware. The items usually have a light blue background. The Nippon pieces were generally produced with a slip trailing decor however, rather than the sprigging ornamentation made popular by Wedgwood. White clay slip was trailed onto the background color of the item by use of tubing or a cone-shaped device to form the pattern.

Yamato: District in central Japan.

Yayoi: People of the bronze and iron culture in Japan dating back to 300 – 100 B.C. They were basically an agricultural people. They made pottery using the potter's wheel.

Yedo: Or Edo, the largest city in Japan, renamed Tokyo, meaning eastern capital.

Yoshihito: Emperor of Japan from 1912 to 1926. He took the name of Taisho which meant "great peace."

Bibliography

A Journal of Fashion, Culture and Fine Arts, Vol. XXXVII. Butterick Publishing Company, London and New York, 1891.

Altick, Richard, D. *Victorian People and Ideas.* W.W. Norton and Company, London, 1973.

Aronson, Theo., *Napoleon and Josephine.* St. Martins Press, 175 Fifth St., New York City, 10010, 1990.

Butler Brothers catalogs, 1906 – 1921.

Ewing. Elizabeth. *History of Twentieth Century Fashion.* Barnes and Noble, Totowa, N.J., 1974, 1986.

Hale, Sarah, J., and Louis A. Godey, editors. *Godey's Lady's Book, Vol. LXXX.* Louis Godey, Philadelphia, 1870.

Hammond, Dorothy. *Mustache Cups.* Wallace-Homestead Book Co., Des Moines, Iowa, 50305, 1972.

Slatkin, Wendy. *Women Artists in History.* Prentice-Hall, Inc., Englewood Cliffs, N.J. 07632.

Stewart, Hilary. *Looking at Indian Art of the Northwest Coast.* University of Washington Press, Seattle, Washington, 1979.

The Aldine. New York, January 1873.

Tuleja, Tad. *Curious Customs.* Harmony Books, division of Crown Publishers, Inc., 225 Park Ave. So., New York City, New York, 1987.

Van Patten, Joan, F. *The Collector's Encyclopedia of Nippon Porcelain.* Collector Books, Paducah, KY, 1979.

——— • *The Collector's Encyclopedia of Nippon Porcelain, Second Series.* Collector Books, Paducah, KY, 1982.

——— • *The Collector's Encyclopedia of Nippon Porcelain, Third Series.* Collector Books, Paducah, KY, 1986.

——— • *The Collector's Encyclopedia of Nippon Porcelain, Fourth Series.* Collector Books, Paducah, KY, 1997.

——— • *The Collector's Encyclopedia of Nippon Porcelain, Fifth Series.* Collector Books, Paducah, KY, 1998.

Van Patten, Joan, F. & Elmer & Peggy Williams. *Celluloid Treasures of the Victorian Era.* Collector Books, Paducah, KY, 1999.

Wells, Richard, D. *Manners Culture and Dress of the Best American Society.* King, Richardson & Co., Publishers, Springfield, Mass., 1891.

Index

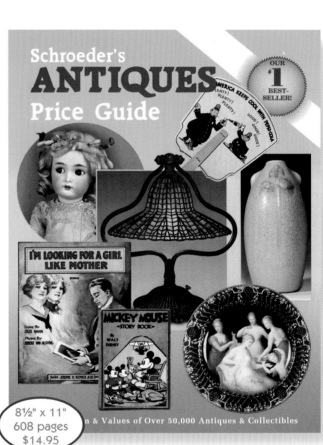